Mike —
Here's to Career
Path Success...

Cheers —

Mark James

MW01288993

KEYS TO THE C SUITE

Unlock the Doors to Executive Career Path Success!

Written By

Mark S. James

Copyright © 2018 Mark James

Published by Branded Expert Publishing

ISBN-13:978-1541119819

ISBN-10:1541119819

Legal Description

All Rights Reserved. No part of this publication may be reproduced in any form or by any means, including scanning, photocopying, or otherwise without prior written permission of the copyright holder.

Disclaimer and Terms of Use: The Author and Publisher have strived to be as accurate and complete as possible in the creation of this book, notwithstanding the fact that they do not warrant or represent at any time that the contents within are accurate due to the rapidly changing nature of the business. While all attempts have been made to verify information provided in this publication, the Author and Publisher assume no responsibility for errors, omissions, or contrary interpretation of the subject matter herein. Any perceived slights of specific persons, peoples, or organizations are unintentional. In practical advice books, like anything else in life, there are no guarantees of income made. Readers are cautioned to rely on their own judgment about their individual circumstances to act accordingly. This book is not intended for use as a source of legal, business, accounting, real estate or financial advice. All readers are advised to seek services of competent professionals in the legal, business, accounting, real estate and finance fields.

Testimonials

"Sound advice for executives who are serious about their career." Marshall Goldsmith, Author of the #1 *New York Times* bestseller - *Triggers*

"Great fundamentals for Middle to Senior Millennials on the Upswing of Their Career!" Dave Opton – Founder, ExecuNet

"Mark James is a true expert, and these are his proven secrets to success...follow them and find your Keys to the C Suite!" Krissi Barr, Author of The Fido Factor and CEO of Barr Corporate Success

"Mark nails the answer to why Job Security is the Ability to Secure the Right Job!" Mark Faust, Author of Growth or Bust and CEO of Echelon Management

"I sort-of knew what needed to be done but was not applying the skills. After hearing Mark talk about it, it helped my understanding of the necessary steps and the right way to start them! He helped me stay focused and held me accountable to my campaign strategy." Tim. M.

"I learned more about my job search in working with you the last 4 months than I have the previous 25 years. I feel you have given me a new boost to my job search and got my career on the right path. All of your sessions helped with what I was missing. You made everything very easy to understand, and I have begun to implement them all - marketing plan, career options, and increased networking." Dave J.

"I was very impressed with the amount of information shared, as well as its quality and relevance. Mark has a very thorough and current knowledge of the national job market. As a result of the excellent preparation and coaching I received, I felt very comfortable and

confident during the interviewing process. When Mark says, 'call me anytime', he means it, and he really wants to hear from you." Chris B.

"My time with Mark helped in several ways. One, it helped to refine my skills and add a little polish to my interviewing. Two, it increased my confidence in interviews, knowing that I had been coached and 'knew the right answers' so to speak. Three, it was helpful to have Mark available as part coach, part cheerleader before some interviews I had. My time with Mark was a great investment in myself." Sue S.

"I was impressed with Mark's knowledge, passion and professionalism. Within 1 month of meeting Mark I was in the hunt for several opportunities. Mark also helped me to negotiate a final offer where I then accepted a great position as Regional Manager with a market leading medical device company. Mark took the fear out of the process and helped me to land well. I would strongly recommend Mark, his services and his company to anyone in a career transition." Randy P.

"Mark, your professional expertise in both executive recruiting and corporate management provided a valuable perspective throughout my job search. I'm certain the length of my search was shortened considerably because of your help. The Job Search Marketing Plan helped me identify my areas of expertise, confirm the value I could bring to a company, and communicate that value to potential employers. Your guidance during our weekly meetings, and prompt response to my phone calls and email messages provided me with a tremendous sense of confidence and the knowledge I was doing everything right." Pam L.

Dedication

To my Father, Daniel H. James, who has been suffering from Alzheimer's for the last 2 decades. In my early days you taught me well, I marveled at your wisdom and the faith you had in me. Your best advice made a big difference and has helped me immeasurably throughout my career: ***"Common Sense is Not So Common"***

Table of Contents

Introduction

My life has not been a bed of roses. I didn't suddenly become an authority in job creation, sales and coaching. It took hard work, mistakes here and there, focus, strategy and growth to be the authority I am today. Going to school, I was an average student. I hated school. I thought my calling was managing and understanding people. I didn't know why the teachers kept giving me tons of assignments when I wasn't any good at it. I believed my degree was in street sense, not book sense; street smart, not book smart. Despite not being good at it, I was determined to do something with my life. I just didn't know what at the time.

My name is Mark S. James, CPC and I have over 25+ years as an Executive Recruiter and Career Management & Transition Coach. As the President of Hire Consulting Services, I am a Certified Personnel Consultant awarded by the National Association of Personnel Services in 1998. I have been the Host and Facilitator of the ExecuNet Meetings in San Diego and Orange County, CA since 2005 and blogging since 2006 as "The Career Catalyst." Yet, all these things are accolades I achieved after a tough journey.

My first real job was at United Parcel Service, where my job description included unloading trucks in 120+ degree temperatures in the summers in Chicago, with dust flying everywhere, including dust from thousands of cardboard boxes. This was only temporary, because I knew it wasn't what I would be doing the rest of my life. Nevertheless, I persevered, got promoted and got out of the trucks into the sort aisle which made it a little easier. Easier meant you had to be great at memorizing every zip code in the country to maintain your primary sorter status. There were 10 different color-coded conveyor belts representing 6 different regions based on all 50 U.S. states. Every month you had to pass a written zip code test and match the zip code with one of ten colors or you could not be a sorter on the primary. If you get more than 10 wrong out of 100 zip codes, then its, *"Get back in the trucks, James!"* At this new sorter position, I did extremely well because I had a good incentive plan. I realized that using my brain was better than increased sweat equity. "Work Smarter – NOT Harder" became my first guiding mindset.

I need you to know something. The fact that you are good at a job doesn't mean that job is perfect for you. I took pride in my work and I excelled to one of the best sorters on the primary, which earned me the opportunity for promotion to a UPS Internal Hub Supervisor. I was managing over 35 Teamster union employees at age 21. Many of my team members were twice my age. There I was, their boss who had barely finished college. That was my early stages of learning how to work, manage and communicate with people in a difficult and fast-paced work environment. I did that for almost five years with UPS.

Moving to California from Chicago back in 1978 was a decision I decided to take if I wanted to grow into my purpose. My first exposure to onboarding people into a new company, or into their first company, was at Gallo Wine Company in Los Angeles. Most of their hires are college recruits right off campus. They bring them to Southern California, the University of Gallo in LA, and they train them. We called them "iron puppies" because they were eager to do anything, and they would work long hours, any time of the day. I learned the ropes quickly and lasted at Gallo for over five years starting as a route sales rep, then promoted in 10 months to take took over supervising my OWN sales team of 8 sales reps as a district manager. It was odd at first - one day I was one of them – the next day I was their boss. A lot of the new hires were being hired and several would be assigned to me or my team and my job would be to train them on how to sell and service retail store locations that sold wine and spirits. At the time, the Gallo Winery boasted that it made and sold 22% of the world's wine. It was big business back when we controlled the wine market – it was also my duty to instill truthful corporate philosophy and be a myth buster with my sales reps and customers.

The boss I had at Gallo was an ex-marine drill sergeant, not terribly likable, but we gave him due respect. Respect was everything and we learned this from the onset. He was tough as nails and he expected perfection from everyone that worked for him. It was a love-like-hate relationship because we knew he was going be tough on us if we messed up. I went from UPS to Gallo thinking, "Oh, this will be a cakewalk," but the Gallo culture is, "Give me five more. Give me 20 more. You better make that quota or you're going to be put on notice." It was a good upbringing, and that helped me understand what discipline, accountability and respect were all about.

From Gallo, it was an upward movement. I was recruited by an executive search firm away from Gallo to work in Orange County, California for Pepsi Cola Bottling Group. I was a district manager and supervised a team composed of 10 sales reps and 10 in-store merchandisers. This was during the 1984 Olympics, and we were competing with Coca-Cola, who had the Olympic sponsorship. We had a lot of perks working for Pepsi: Angels and Dodgers baseball tickets, Lakers tickets and we even had Michael Jackson concert tickets, which was a real big thing back then. Grocery store managers had to be "incentivized" to keep up our store presence. It wasn't really a sales job per se, but more of a "commodity recognition and achievements" job responsibility. If you didn't have display floor space and isle end caps at supermarkets, then your product didn't move as fast as it should. If your competition was taking those end caps, then they were going to outsell you every time. That was a great business lesson for me.

As I look back, my earlier positions helped formulate where I am today, from knowing what it takes to get the job done to having the determination and the no-quit tenacious attitude. That's what matters most in career path development and management. I think that helped me, even before I knew it, to become a successful career coach, executive recruiter, consultant, entrepreneur and leader in the making. That was and continues to be my motivation to being the best.

If you're stuck in a dead-end job, afraid to transition into something bigger and better, not knowing what your next move should be, or just terrified going on job interviews, then I have the solutions for you. At one time I was in the same boat that you are in. But from years of listening, observing, and trial and error, I finally found the Keys to the C Suite. If you are ready to unlock the doors of uncertainty, fear and confusion, please read on. You're just one key away from success!

Mark S. James

Chapter 1

My Transition

A wise man once said, *"Do not stop until you get to your destination."* In the journey towards getting to the peak of my career, I kept moving. The next stop I made was at Polaroid. Polaroid presented new opportunities. It was a fun period because we had unique, highly accepted products that people treated like a novelty, like the Polaroid One-Step. They sold millions of Polaroid One-Step camera and at the time Polaroid took their entire sales force to Bermuda for their national sales meeting. They were doing extremely well, and we were enjoying the benefits.

Enterprise is a wonderful thing. If you have a system that works and people who love it, then they're going to want it. Meeting client expectations and receiving instant client gratification was a skill I learned at Polaroid. I also learned that the real world goes like this: When you're hired to sell, you fail to see beyond your targets.

We gave away cameras and we made tons of money on the film. We called it the "razor and the razor blade" system of selling; you give them the razor, but they have to buy the blades, and the blade is the most profitable item... just like the film was the most profitable item at Polaroid.

As a Sales and Marketing Representative, my territory was the I-10 freeway from Hollywood out to Palm Springs.

To increase sales, I ran a value-added tie-in promotion with the Bob Hope Desert Classic Golf Tournament and Longs Drugs (Now CVS). The deal was when you bought a Polaroid Camera, you received two free tickets to the Bob Hope Desert Classic Golf Tournament. That promotion sold a ton of cameras and a LOT of very profitable Polaroid Film. Customer entertainment was the key.

From experiences like these, I grew a whole new appreciation for marketing - the lifeblood of sales. If you don't have a good marketing plan, then you're dead in the water. I learned that if you want to market yourself, you have to be able to tell your stories and examples of your career accomplishments, successes and proudest achievements. You're not selling; you're telling your anecdotal stories that are bullets on your resume, which then come alive in a job interview. To reach the C Suite, you need to be able to market yourself.

Soon after the Bob Hope Desert Classic Golf Tournament promotion, Polaroid moved me to San Diego, the Jewel of the Pacific. That move started to design my life and career even more. The key to the door of the Universal Law of Serendipity was opened.

I ended up living next to an executive recruiter and we became friends. He said, "You'd be great as a recruiter. I just think you've got the gift." I started to think about it when I went on sales recognition award trips to the beaches in Maui. I said to myself "You know what? It's time for me to get out of consumer package goods and really start embracing a service industry type job." Instead of tangible sales, I took the challenge and started doing an intangible sale - executive recruiting.

Later, I found that recruiting is one of the most difficult jobs out there.

In recruiting, you have to close a company and you have to close a candidate in order to make a placement. It's the same thing with regards to selling a house as a realtor. You have to close a seller and a buyer. So, it's a multiple type sell, two different entities, or three, including yourself, and it must be win, win, win or you are not closing the deal.

I was passed over for the position of District Manager at Polaroid, so now it was just a matter of time before I moved into the next phase of my life and career. That said, you have to undergo the process of acquiring knowledge and training to achieve your goals, so that was what I did. Through my training, I moved on to work with Management Recruiters International, commonly known as MRI, and at that time it was thought of as the IBM or Xerox of recruiting. At MRI, I was introduced to the wisdom of Jim Rohn and his treasury of motivational quotes: *"If you don't design your own life plan, chances are you'll fall into someone else's plan. And guess what they have planned for you? Not much."*

Having phone presence with voice inflection, listening skills, asking tough questions, waiting and pausing for answers are the big skills I learned through systematic practice. Doing one thing over and over again to get the best results. I didn't have a love affair with recruiting, but it was a good way to earn a living. However, I found myself stuck in an office on the phone every day and missing consumer package goods once again.

Answering a newspaper ad back in 1989, the year I got married, I became a technical sales and service representative for the AGFA Photo Division of Miles Laboratories, which later became Bayer Corporation. It was a great job I held for seven years. I distinctly remember that I got the job because I was really persistent.

In this role, I had an expanded territory: all of New Mexico, Arizona, Southern Nevada, and Southern California, from San Diego up to Orange County. It was a big territory and we were upselling film against Kodak. AGFA Film, made in Germany, was the best portrait film in the world - ideal for natural colors and skin tones. Now here I am once again, selling consumer packaged goods to camera shops, food and drug stores and distributors in the Southwest U.S. I had a wonderful territory. Who wouldn't love working in the Southwest United States covering Southern California, Arizona, Nevada and New Mexico? I could jump on a plane for $39 one way, be in a town one morning and another one the next morning. I was selling up a storm and living it up. I loved that job, so I excelled at it and was promoted to Director of National Accounts and moved to Cincinnati, Ohio in 1992 with my wife and daughter. Things were great. We bought a nice house, blended in with all the neighbors, even though we were transients from far away in San Diego. Four years later AGFA wanted me to move to New Jersey or I didn't have a job. They told me, "Sorry, but you either move to New Jersey or you're out. There's no job for you, Mark." Has anyone told you something like this before? Have you ever been in a situation where you have dedicated 7+ years of your life grooming a business and just when you want to stretch your legs, the rug is yanked out from under you? I knew that if I moved to New Jersey, that would be the end of my life and my marriage. We had come all the way from California, to Ohio and we weren't going to move further east.

There are many reasons why executives are on the move. Hundreds of jobs get eliminated every day. Most times, a company promotion almost always includes a move to keep your job, which is exactly what happened when I accepted my promotion and relocation package from San Diego to Cincinnati. But I realized that enough was enough. Moving to New Jersey was not in the cards and it was time to once again take charge of my life and career.

Therefore, I chose door #2, took the severance and outplacement benefit services and never worked at a big corporation ever again.

My outplacement experience was exactly what I needed. My contract was with Drake Beam and Morin (DBM), which was acquired by Lee Hecht Harrison, a global outplacement firm. From this experience, I learned what career transition coaching was all about first hand. I knew

4

someday I wanted to make coaching a part of my career path. At the time, I had no idea how much of an impact that would have on me.

The transition out of the AGFA and, more so, out of corporate America, kept me at a loss about what to do next. With the early formulation of my belief system in recruiting, and the urging of my assigned coach at DBM, John "Ike" Eichelberg, I decided to get back into the service industry of executive search. I interviewed with several search firms in Cincinnati, eventually getting offered a great job and Vice President of Sales with The Angus Group, a boutique retained search firm with over 33 years in business. As a recruiter at a very reputable search firm in a small town, you tend to get very popular.

Overall, creating my own company came as a result of my transition out of corporate America.

People kept coming to me saying, "You're really good at this. Can you look at my resume? I've got a big interview tomorrow." Friends and family became a big part of my vision and epiphany. When formulating my business' services, I added career transition coaching to the menu of services in addition to recruiting. Owning my own business is the dream job, or at least that's what it became for me because I love what I do. As the saying goes, you never work a day in your life if you love what you do. I'm doing it right now and I love it.

Chapter 2

The Ultimate Power Is to Know Thyself

Before you wade into the competitive executive labor market, one question you need to ask yourself is: *Do I know myself?* If you genuinely know your strengths, competencies and natural talents, you can be very effective in an interview. Socrates, the great philosopher, taught that knowing oneself is the ultimate power. Career competencies are a set of natural abilities that have been developed through formal or non-formal education, work experience and behavior needed to effectively perform a job function. Core competencies are required for all role profiles, which can be leveraged widely to many products, services, markets, industries and companies.

On the next few pages are surveys and worksheets that help you define the kind of person you are, and the competencies, strengths and skills you possess. Circle or highlight those words that best describe you and the image you wish to make to your next employer. Feel free to write in any other descriptive words or skills that may help clarify who you are. Think: What is your highest and best use to an organization? What do you do better than anyone on this side of the equator? What are your greatest deliverables?

Then list your Top 8 competencies and strengths i.e.: Energetic, Achievement Oriented, Motivation, Detail Oriented, Adaptable, Resourceful, Dedicated, Creative Thinking, Strategic, Resourceful, Focused, etc.

Achievement Oriented	Clear/Rapid Reactions	Multi-tasking assignments
Aggressive	Diligence/Persistence	Adaptability/Flexibility
Ambitious	Dedication/Loyalty	Creative/Innovative
Desire to Succeed	Experienced/Seasoned	Detail Oriented
Energetic	Organizational Ability	Efficient Work
Focused	Learning Quickly	Planning/Conceptual Skills
Go Getter	Strong Accomplishments	Project Oriented
Hard Worker	Well Rounded	Reliable
Motivated	Versatile	Patience
Results Oriented	Facilitator	Resourceful
Commitment to Excellence	Creative Thinking	Analytically Oriented
Confident Decision Making	Tenacious	Dedicated Team Player
Honesty/Integrity	Solution Provider	Entrepreneurial Persistence
Bottom-line driven	Respected by Others	Innovative
Self-Management	Responsible	Leadership Skills
Visualization	Positive Attitude	Dynamic
Outcome-based	Committed to Excellence	Clear Communicator
Reasoning	Precise/Detailed	Enjoys a Challenge
Strategic	Efficient/Effective Actions	Problem Solver
Solution Provider	Resilient	Focused

First, List Your Top 8 Competencies/Strengths Below:

1.

2.

3.

4.

5.

6.

7.

8.

Next, Create Your Own Career Acronym

Now take the first letter of each prioritized competency and strength and create your own acronym by inserting each letter in a box below.

Lastly, Memorize Your Acronym

Memorize this group of 8 letters to recall your competencies and strengths quickly during an interview, phone screen or networking conversation or meeting.

Tip: Develop stories and examples about your 8 competencies and strengths that describe a **C.A.R statement: Challenge + Action = Result.** These stories and examples are your accomplishments (Action=Result) that are outlined as bullet points on your resume. During your interview, talk about the **"Challenge"** and **HOW** you did it. Note: The challenge could be a problem, obstacle, goal, issue, deadline, quota, initiative or crisis.

Skills Inventory

Circle or highlight all the skills that describe yourself and indicate your highest and best use in all categories. Then select your top 12 choices, as you did in the competency and strength section on the previous page.

PEOPLE SKILLS

Building Rapport/Relationships

Communication/Interpersonal Skills

Resolving Client Concerns

Keeping Staff Turnover Low

Project Development

Evaluating Employee Performance

Improving Productivity

Problem Resolution

Supervisory Skills

Time Management

OTHER GENERAL SKILLS

Writing/Editing

Motivating Others

OPERATIONS / MANAGEMENT

Attention to Customer Service Bookkeeping

Administration Benefits/Payroll

Developing Business Strategies/Expense Control

Direct Mail & Telemarketing/Detailed Analysis

Developing Startup Businesses/Bank Reconciliation's

Interviewing Others/Financial Management

Entrepreneurialism/Organization/Record Keeping

General Accounting Knowledge/General Ledger

Policy Formulation

Market Assessment

Negotiation

Careful Research/Analysis

Keys to the C Suite

COMMUNICATION

Strong Follow Up	P & L Responsibilities	Meeting Aggressive Schedules
Product Development/Introduction	Performance Evaluations	Working with All Ability Levels
Proven Achievement Record	Productivity Improvement	Advertising/Public Relations
Market Analysis/Research	Public Relations	Dedication/Commitment
Presentation Skills	Quality Control Needs	Assessments/Evaluations
Referral Development	Recruiting	Creative Program Development
Creative Sales Approaches	Staff Supervision	Computer Skills
Large Account/National Sales	Training & Development	Continuing Education
Merchandising	Troubleshooting	Relationship Building
New Market Identification	Maintaining High Standards	
Operations Management	Creating Positive Enthusiasm	
Cold Calling	Verbal/Written Skills	
Handling Rejection Positively		

ACCOUNTING / FINANCE

Maintaining High Standards

Continuing Business Education

General Accounting/Finance	Patience & Encouragement	
Top Management Interaction	Financial Statements	Clearly Explaining Concepts
Account Development	Accurately Analyzing Behavior	Successful Account Protection
Superior Communication	Auditing / Inventory Management	Delegating Authority
Resolving Client Concerns	Accounts Payable/Receivable Inventory/Office Management	

Now, List Your Top 12 Skills Below:

1.

2.

3.

4.

5.

6.

7.

8.

9.

10.

11.

12.

TIP: Make sure you insert these skills (keywords) in a table under your career summary (profile) at the top of your resume. These skills can be tailored (add or subtract) to your audience, target industries and companies.

Executive Level Management Expertise Competencies:

Choose your personal management level and record your chosen level on Page 19. Then (without peeking on Page 20) calculate your total points and see where you rank. Be honest – this will help you determine where your leadership growth opportunities are.

1. Change Management/Orientation

Definition: Managing resources and interrelationships to achieve successful implementation of change processes and strategies.

Level 1 - Gives commitment and involves self in the change process. Contributes to change strategies.

Level 2 - Involves all parties in own area of responsibility and encourage their commitment to the change project. Contributes to change strategies.

Level 3 - Takes responsibility and ownership for change processes and strategies, in more than one area of change. Manages people through stages of change.

Level 4 - Separates self to provide an overview for the change in its larger context. Manages conflict caused by change. Develops and implements change strategies and provides direction.

2. Consultative Approach

Definition: Adopting a style of decision-making that allows for input of others, considering the impact of decisions and keeping others informed.

Level 1 - Open to input from other key players before making decisions.

Level 2 - Establishes the need for and the degree of consultation required; seeks input from a range of key stakeholders; informs all involved of the decision made.

Level 3 - Major decision making, seeking input from all relevant internal/external stakeholders to ensure all aspects of the decision are thoroughly considered.

Level 4 - Employs astute political judgment to involve all relevant stakeholders in major decisions; recognizes multiple agendas and makes/communicates final decision in ways that foster maximum ownership and minimum resistance.

3. Delegation

Definition: Delegating tasks or responsibilities providing adequate instruction and resources and managing the progress.

Level 1 - Delegates routine work, ensuring adequate instruction and monitors progress.

Level 2 - Delegates substantial tasks, selecting staff, providing instructions and managing progress.

Level 3 - Delegates responsibility and accountability for major work and decision making, based on clear criteria of staff competency and interest.

Level 4 - Delegates and monitors progress of broad objectives to a team with diverse skills.

4. Developing People

Definition: Placing importance on developing others and using a range of strategies to enhance peoples' performance.

Level 1 - Provides direction on correct performance of tasks and assigns challenging tasks that will help people develop their skills.

Level 2 - Provides timely constructive feedback and coaching that facilitates improvement and builds self-esteem.

Level 3 - Actively coaches direct reports in how to get the most learning from an assignment. This also encourages people to invest their time in relevant training.

Level 4 - Systematically promotes development of people by holding others accountable for competency enhancement; provides a range of assignments and invests resources for learning.

5. Empowering Others

Definition: Communicating trust and confidence in others, spurring them to exercise initiative and take responsibility.

Level 1 - Clearly outlines what is required for routine, defined tasks; clarifies levels of responsibility and accountability; conveys confidence in staff's ability to succeed.

Level 2 - Outlines expected results for complex tasks, responsibility and accountability; sanctions independent, autonomous action within specific boundaries.

Level 3 - Sanctions others taking calculated, informed risks in less defined situations; ensures all stakeholders are aware of the responsibility/accountability given to staff.

Level 4 - Allocates responsibility and accountability in line with staff competency in highly complex or ambiguous situations; encourages informed risk-taking; encourages others to provide solutions, not just identify problems.

6. Hands-On Approach

Definition: Maintains current knowledge and interest in activities of direct reports or functional areas and is accessible to assist direct reports with problems.

Level 1 - Demonstrates current working knowledge of relevant issues in own area of accountability.

Level 2 - Accessible to staff within area of accountability, irrespective of position; keeps up-to-date with activities of own area and dynamics and other relevant areas.

Level 3 - Develops and maintains a system of communication and activity, which enables being kept in touch without detracting from achieving strategic accountabilities.

Level 4 - Acts as role model for other leaders in maintaining an in-depth awareness of own area and others; demonstrates good working knowledge of current issues in areas with strategic links to own.

7. Leading Motivating Teams

Definition: Using appropriate interpersonal styles and methods to inspire and guide individuals or groups towards goal achievement.

Level 1 - Engenders a sense of unity and teamwork. Works within a team to lead and motivate through shared leadership.

Level 2 - Communicates a sense of direction. Guides others to meet those agendas. Leads from the front in small to medium areas of responsibility. Encourages others to work together towards a common goal.

Level 3 - Determines and directs agendas for others. Leads by collaboration and facilitating own large groups and areas of responsibility. Demonstrates awareness of how to use other leadership styles.

Level 4 - Leads by example. Provides clear expectations and direction. This causes people to believe what they do makes a difference. It uses different leadership styles effectively to achieve objectives.

8. Performance Management

Definition: Setting clear goals; assigning responsibilities; measuring performance and managing feedback to achieve quality and timely results.

Level 1 - Identifies clear targets and objectives for own position and establishes methods for measurement and feedback.

Level 2 - Establish mutual objectives and targets for own team members; develops and maintains system for team performance measurement and feedback.

Level 3 - Provides clear feedback on performance on a formal and informal basis; empowers staff to take corrective action; develops an environment that creates positive behavior change, rewards and acknowledges success.

Level 4 - Instills a performance-based culture when required, takes disciplinary action in ways that minimize adverse circumstances, emphasizes mutual respect and secures the best outcome for the organization.

9. Tough-Mindedness

Definition: Standing firm when making decisions or carrying out action even when these are unpopular.

Level 1 - Communicates own viewpoint and opinion in clear terms to immediate team.

Level 2 - Clearly articulates own position to team members and others; stands by this in the face of opposition in adverse or difficult settings.

Level 3 - Makes tough decisions that are in the best interests of the business without procrastinating or succumbing to undue pressure.

Level 4 - Astute in making and standing by decisions that will serve the long-term interests of the business despite encountering strong resistance. Manages the communication and implementation of these decisions to counter opposition and maximize acceptance.

10. Visionary

Definition: Creating a vision or direction for the team, which is both compelling and challenging and inspiring others to work towards it.

Level 1 - Contributes to the vision of the team. Works collaboratively towards it.

Level 2 - Outlines a clear direction for team members and motivates them towards important goals.

Level 3 - Articulates a clear strategic vision, generates enthusiasm in others and implements strategy to gain the support of people in the department or organization.

Level 4 - Creates a compelling vision that breaks new ground; constantly communicates the strategic vision and is a role model for energizing others to work towards that vision.

Record and total your executive management expertise level ranking below for each competency:

1. **Change Management/Orientation:** _____

2. **Consultative Approach:** _____

3. **Delegation:** _____

4. Developing People: _____

5. Empowering Others: _____

6. Hands-On Approach: _____

7. Leading/Motivating Team: _____

8. Performance Management: _____

9. Tough-Mindedness: _____

10. Visionary: _____

Total: _____

Keys to Management Level Point Rankings

10-15 Points = Junior to Middle-Level Management

16-25 Points = Middle to Director Level Management

26-35 Points = Vice President to Senior Executive VP

35-40 Points = President to C Suite

The key to this management level ranking exercise is to learn your leadership style, decision-making process, beliefs and philosophy. Once you have selected your current level, begin to implement and use your chosen descriptions to express yourself in meetings, interviews and networking conversations. Remember, you can aspire to raise your ranking to the next level as you progress in your management role, responsibilities and accountabilities.

Chapter 3

Job Security is the Ability to Secure a Job

Here are some statistics that will blow your mind:

- The average 40-year-old has changed jobs 10 times. (every 18-38 months = 2.3 years)
- 1M people turn age 60 every year in U.S.
- 15,000 people celebrate their 65th birthday – EVERY DAY!
- 69% of U.S. companies have less than 100 employees.
- 60% of people do 2 things after losing their job:
    1. Call friends and family
    2. Get on the job boards and post their resume

- 85% of all jobs are never advertised!!!!!
- Most job seekers have no job search plan at all!
- 1 out 20 people have gone through interview training
- Most job seekers are unrealistic of job market in relation to their skills!

Why you need help with your resume

A resume is much more than a statement listing all your work experience and achievements. A lot of people have come to me for the first time with no clue of what they should add on their resumes, aside from what Google says. In many of these situations, some of them have never had to look for a job. Perhaps, it has been one friend saying, "Come on over here for the most of your career." Then they jump on board. What happens is that when it finally stops, that little wheel of referral or the need for someone to go and jump ship and go to another company, they end up outside of the box, so to speak, with all the deck chairs being rearranged. In many cases, their resume has been poorly developed, and they don't even have a LinkedIn profile. I'm talking of senior executives that have been cocooning in their job, really busy, working, doing wonderful things and then it just stops. And then they're lost, they're like a cork on the ocean. I always say that you don't want to get stuck in a sinking boat, too busy bailing and no time to row ashore. Can you relate?

L.U.C.K.

The word "LUCK has been misused by many to mean getting things one ordinarily didn't work for. A lot of people think you must have luck to get a new job, right? To me, there's a certain amount of luck that happens when you are in the right place at the right time, getting out of bed and going to the right event where you get a handshake and you meet somebody that turns out to be a referral to a business owner and the connection turns into an interview and you get an offer and you start a new job. Boom! The old saying is Preparation + Opportunity = LUCK. I say, **"LUCK** stands for *Laboring Under Correct Knowledge."*

You have to make your own luck. It's that universal law of serendipity that I talk about that provides a pathway of choices and each choice you make is another path leading to another path. It starts with hitting the snooze button on your alarm and getting out of bed - or getting out of bed right away and increasing your job search activity! This means networking and connecting with people, real people in person, face to face meetings. This is the number one thing that has to happen in a job search campaign. It starts with a phone call and then you confirm it with an email.

Want To Get Lucky? Note: This was adapted from an article in Fast Company magazine.

These 4 Principles Can Create Good Fortune in your Life and Career:

1. Maximize Chance Opportunities - Lucky people are skilled at

creating, noticing and acting upon chance opportunities. They do this in various ways, which include building and maintaining a strong network, adopting a relaxed attitude to life and being open to new experiences.

2. **Listen to Your Lucky Hunches** - Lucky people make effective decisions by listening to their intuition and gut feelings. They also take steps to actively boost their intuitive abilities and clearing their mind of negative thoughts.

3. **Expect Good Fortune** - Lucky people are certain the future will be bright. Over time, that expectation becomes a self-fulfilling prophecy because it helps lucky people persist in the face of failure and positively shapes their interactions with other people.

4. **Turn Bad Luck into Good** - Lucky people employ various psychological techniques to cope with, and even thrive upon, the ill fortune that comes their way. For example, they spontaneously imagine how things could have been worse, they don't dwell on the ill fortune, and they take control of the situation.

7 Daily Tips for Being Highly Productive to Get You Focused and On Track

1. Work backward from goals to milestones to tasks. Writing down "secure 3 first interviews in 60 days" at the top of your to-do list is a sure way to make sure you never get it done. Break down the work into smaller and smaller chunks until you have specific tasks that can be accomplished in a few hours or days: Sketch a detailed outline with critical success factors and actions to achieving this goal. That's how you set goals and actually succeed in crossing them off your list.

2. Stop multi-tasking. No, seriously—stop. Switching from task to task quickly does not work. In fact, changing tasks more than 10 times in a

day makes you less effective. When you multitask, your IQ actually drops by an average of 10 points, 15 for men, five for women (yes, men are three times as bad at multitasking than women).

3. Stay disciplined and eliminate distractions. Lock your door, put a sign up, turn off your phone, texts, email, and instant messaging. In fact, if you know you may sneak a peek at your email, set it to offline mode, or even turn off your internet connection. Go to a quiet area and focus on completing one task at a time.

4. Schedule your email. Pick two or three times during the day when you're going to use your email. Checking your email constantly throughout the day creates a ton of noise and kills your productivity.

5. Use the phone. Email isn't meant for conversations, plus it can be impersonal and easily dismissed. Don't reply more than twice to an original email. Get off the computer - pick up the phone instead to schedule face-to-face meetings and get out of the house.

6. Work on your own agenda. Don't let something else set your day. Most people go right to their emails and start freaking out. Sure, you will end up with an empty inbox, but nothing important will be accomplished. After you wake up, drink water so you rehydrate, eat a good breakfast to replenish your glucose and set prioritized goals for the rest of your day. Tip: if possible, take a 45-minute nap in a low lighted room for extra energy in the afternoon.

7. Work in 60 to 90-minute intervals. Your brain uses up more glucose than any other bodily activity. Typically, you will have spent most of it after 60-90 minutes. (That's why you feel so burned out after super long meetings.) So, take a break: Get up, go for a walk, have a snack, do something completely different to recharge. And? Yes, that means you need an extra hour for breaks, not including lunch, so if you're required

to get eight hours of work done each day, plan to be there for 9 to 10 hours.

"Life and career success comes from good judgment. Good judgment comes from experience. Experience comes from bad judgment."

In today's market, the only job security is your ability to secure a job! If you are having problems getting results during your search, consider hiring a professional career transition coach!

Why you need the help of a professional to land a good job

As a senior executive wading into the pool of unemployment, you need the help of a professional to find a job at your level. There is the need for someone in your corner that can give you a perspective on things and keep you from these highs and lows. You need to choose someone that knows what they're doing and even then, go through a list of all the credentials you have, just so that it's obvious that you are qualified for the job that will come your way.

Let's say you got called and you just found out that you have been right sized. What's the very first thing you would ask professional or ask him to do? The first thing you need to realize is that in today's market, people want a professional working with them to help them find a job. It's the most effective way to get things done without breaking a sweat.

Where a career transition coach comes in is as a master of sorts. They're the person that's the thought leader, the expert with the knowledge and wisdom of what it takes to conduct a professional job search campaign. In this field of ours, it is ideal to have an outside perspective. As a career transition coach myself, I've had experience working with many different companies and executives and I have seen and heard a lot. As a job seeker, you are limited to only the experience where you were in your career and your subordinate's careers. Knowing how the process works makes you beat it.

It's not a great feeling to be behind a job and have no fulfillment. That feeling of "I deserve more." Through my experience as a coach, I have been behind their eyes - I know what they see, and I know that feeling of frustration and maybe even panic. People have a mortgage. They have kids in college. These are the senior executives, but anyone that has financial obligations has that pressure. There's an emotional rollercoaster when you're in a transition between opportunities.

Imagine this scenario about an interview: Let's say you get an interview and you get really excited. Your spirits are way up, and it doesn't go anywhere. All of a sudden, your spirits are diving like a plane into the ground because of the fear and uncertainty. The highs and lows, peaks and valleys. Here is what I would suggest for the good of your health. Don't get too high and don't get too low. Don't get too excited, and certainly don't get too depressed because that's when the doubt and the denial and the thought of, "Am I really good enough?" starts to creep in. A state of denial is one of the worst things that people can get, and it's tough to pull them out of that. If this shows at an interview, the prospective employers will be able to sense this from a mile away.

As a coach, the emotional rollercoaster is the first thing I try to determine in my prospective clients. Understanding what their current status in their life is, in their mind, in their world and what their attitude is like. Attitude, like author of *The 7 Habits of Highly Effective People* Stephen Covey said, "It's 10% what happened to you and 90% is decided by how you react to it as far as the circumstance."

Job searching typically starts with a really positive attitude. If somebody calls or somebody you meet at an event says, "Hey, Mark, how are you doing?" And I say, "I'm fine." You know what fine means? **F.I.N.E. means Freaked out, Inferior, Neurotic, and Emotional.**

By being fearful, and not finding a job they desire, they end up losing money and burning a burn rate, because they don't have a revenue stream coming in. Then the fear factor kicks in and they start fearing the worst... and, of course, we know **F.E.A.R.** means **False Evidence (or Expectations) Appearing Real.**

I know how these things feel. Although the only time I ever got fired was when a union came in and found I was underage, my experience includes others who have been close to me. I've seen my friends go through it where they had huge self-doubts and worried about their own worth and that sort of thing. It takes so many months per 10,000 to find a job and the longer you're out, the less you're worth. There's all kinds of myths that you're much more familiar with, some are true, and some aren't.

Referrals

There are millions of jobs available a month but the higher you go on the employment pyramid, the fewer the opportunities. Senior executives are chasing only a few thousand out of the millions. Therefore, referrals are very important.

Referrals give you a slight edge over the other person who is also out for a particular job. Sometimes, the toughest thing to do is to land a new job not because you are not qualified, but because people want someone already familiar with the system. Most of these operational people are homegrown and are brought up through the system. It is difficult for a company to bring somebody in from the outside unless it's a known entity, somebody who's internally saying, "This is the guy we need." If you have not networked yourself to this circle, how will you be recommended? It all starts with relationships. No matter what we are trying to do or whatever we are trying to accomplish in life or career, it all happens with the handshake and the warm introductions. That's it.

In this instance, it's not about who you know, but who knows you. It is also about what they're saying about you. That's the new paradigm; the new paradigm of having accolades and connections talking you up in circles without you being there. You know, the "You need to call John. John Doe is your man." You don't even know that you're going to get that intro because someone else is talking about you and it's because you've made an impression on that person. In some cases, you were able to tell your story, and that person understands how your journey relates. "The difference between Not Working and Networking is ONE letter."

Starting a conversation

I was a guest speaker on a panel with two other individuals presenting to about 150 people in La Jolla, California. It was organized for people either in transition or planning to make a change or executives and consultants that are currently working that want to learn how to manage their career path more effectively. As a result of that speaking engagement, I got an email from a gentleman who just got released from his company and he wanted to see if I had time to talk on the phone or have a cup of coffee. It was his request. My immediate response to him if he came up to me at the event would have been "Of course!", but he didn't get a chance and now his email got lost among the rest. If the chance is presented to you, a face-to-face interaction will always be more memorable than an email.

Don't try to get immediate gratification by emailing everybody to try to get things set up. You need to call them, get the conversation started, and then email is wonderful for confirming everything once you've agreed on a meeting or a call. At a minimum, a phone call is essential and then the goal being leading to a face-to-face meeting over a cup of coffee or an ice tea or a lunch or dinner.

No matter the communication choice, meeting with a coach is a great step to take, but the preparation doesn't stop there! When meeting with someone in career transition, my goal is to talk first on the phone, have a quick introduction and then set up a time to meet in person, if possible, or via webcam. It also helps both parties to send in your resume or LinkedIn web page so that the coach knows who they're talking to or meeting with before the two meet. I want to know a little of who you are beforehand, so we can have the most productive meeting.

Getting Face to Face

Nothing is more important than face-to-face meetings. There is no substitute for getting a handshake followed by real in-person dialogue. Here are mistakes that can prevent this meeting from being successful:

Mistake #1: Talking about Yourself—All the Time

Mistake #2: Expecting a Job

Mistake #3: Failure to Know How to Tell Your Story

Mistake #4: You Are a Nobody That No One Sent

Mistake #5: Not Saying Thank-you

Mistake #6: Forgetting to Follow Up <u>Quickly</u>

The Critical Importance of Following Up

After your face-to-face meeting, networking event, mixer, association meeting, seminar, conference or trade show – what happens the next day? Do you follow up with people you just met – like you promised to do OR were asked to do?

TIP: Don't forget to research the person in advance and connect with them on LinkedIn! Send a personal note in your LinkedIn connection request reminding the contact of where you met and insert your best contact phone number and email. Suggest an appointment call on the phone to set up a time to meet over coffee, breakfast or lunch for a one-on-one meeting.

Before a network event or meeting, do your due diligence: Research who's going to be there, know the dress code, and prepare a self-introduction that's relevant to the event. You know that this will be a great opportunity to expand your network. Then you attend the event and meet a handful of new, potentially-valuable contacts, all of whom will be assets to your network, and many of which you know who you will be able to help. All in all, this was one of your more successful networking events, and you leave feeling pretty good about yourself. *Now What?*

The critical mistake is not following up with the new contacts you've made. The word "work" is in networking for a reason. Remember – you don't go to a networking event simply to have a good time or because you're hungry or thirsty. You attend for various reasons; you are in career transition or you are representing your company to explore and meet new connections. To make the most out of your networking experience, it's imperative that the follow-up occurs within 48 hours, while the memory of connecting is new and fresh!

Here is a list of key actions to help you follow-up more effectively:

• **Collecting Business Cards –** Collecting business cards is, of course, the first order of business. Never assume that other people will follow-up with you just because you gave them your card.

• **Time Management -** When you've confirmed your attendance at an event, schedule the time in your day to follow up! Many times, people do not follow up because they get busy, they forget, life takes over, they are lazy, or they don't really care.

•**Takes Notes on the Business Card** - While the information is fresh, be sure to write notes on every card. What was said? What was the focus? What can you do for that person? What angle should you take for your follow-up? Staying organized in this manner is critical, especially if you connected with many new individuals.

• **Connect by Email (Within 48 Hours)** - According to a recent study, an office worker can receive an average of 121 emails per day. Remember to keep in mind your approach for each follow-up – a generic message to everyone isn't a good idea. You want it to be personal, meaningful and relative, and the message should reflect what was discussed during your brief conversation.

• **Persistence Is important** - Follow up your email with a phone call. Leave a voicemail if necessary. If you don't receive a call back or email reply within a week, be patient as there are plenty of good reasons why other people can't or don't follow up with you. Lastly, call the person again with the hopes of catching them live on the phone to have a brief chat.

Above all, don't take it personal or get emotional because of their delay or ignorance. Follow up at least three times before you give up. Allow a week or two in between your messages so that you don't look like your harassing the person. Just like in baseball, three strikes and you're out. Bottom Line: It's important to remember that most people are extremely busy, yet that's no excuse for their rudeness or lack of consideration. Try not to take it personally. Instead of fretting about it, just move on and concentrate on cultivating business with clients who value and respect you.

• **TIP: I saw this and thought of you…** When it comes time to maintain the connection you took the time to establish, pass on a memo with the tagline "I saw this and thought of you…" It could be a piece of mail, a text, an email or even a mention in a tweet. This is a great one when reading an interesting online article, blog or post. The only reason I read the news is to use that information to follow up my network, clients and customers.

Chapter 4

Job Search Marketing Plan

"Hidden jobs are hidden only from those who have their heads stuck in the internet job postings."

The job search campaign is more than just having a resume and a LinkedIn profile. You need a blueprint for success, which I call a Job Search Marketing Plan, or **JSMP**.

Conducting a professional job search campaign has many pitfalls. There are no shortcuts in job search. There is no magic answer. Many variables can stop the entire hiring process. It all starts with, number one, having a plan and number two, executing the plan. When the execution goes well, you're going to get a first interview.

The JSMP is your job search strategy. It consists of Job Objective, Positioning Statement (referred to as a 2-minute elevator speech) and Exit Statement (reason for leaving your job). This document contains your TOP 8 competencies and examples of your career accomplishments. The JSMP defines exactly what you are looking for in the next job. It has three unique industries with 20 target companies you have researched listed under each industry. A JSMP is what exactly constitutes the ideal job in maybe 10-12 bullets from size of company, number of employees, annual revenue and location. It goes down to what color the wallpaper is in your office. Do you have a window in your corner office? Do you have your own parking spot? Whatever is important to you, it needs to be defined and decided upon. After this, we examine the landscape. The landscape is how many of these potential companies are out there that could yield this type of a job that you have outlined. If there's only three or four of these companies in your zip code, then you have to expand the landscape. If relocation is not an option, it limits your choices. In job search, it's all about having more choices.

However, the planning of that has to happen first. A lot of people just jump into the fire and start networking without messaging. They don't have their resume ready, their LinkedIn profile is not optimized properly, and they don't have an answer to, "What are you looking for in the ideal job? "Oh, I'm kind of open." You tell that to a recruiter and the recruiter's going to say, "You figure it out, and then call me back." It drives me crazy when someone says, "I'm industry agnostic and I'm good at a lot of things." This type of vague answer doesn't help anyone." You need to able to help me – Help you!

Readjust Your Expectations

Some of the things you have heard about job seeking are myths! Most people will tell you to keep searching on the internet if you want a new job. That's like throwing your net into an ocean with no idea if it will catch any fish. There are several habits you must undertake if you want to be effective at conducting a professional job search campaign:

- **Hire a professional career transition coach**

Professional career coaches provide expert advice with unbiased opinions and "knowledge transfer" to their clients throughout the entire job search process. They train each client to develop essential skills in networking, interviewing, and salary negotiation. Some coaches will provide professional introductions to help their clients expand their network and connectivity to key executives and professionals. A career coach provides the necessary emotional support to get their clients through the job transition. Above all, a career coach will hold their clients accountable and keep them focused to achieve critical weekly activity goals. Hiring a good career coach will typically speed up the job search process and can save you weeks and months of time-wasting mistakes. The main role of a career coach is to take on each client as a student and teach them to be the master. When you go through structured career coaching you are equipped to manage the rest of your career. When you find yourself in career transition again, you will know exactly what to do with a solid foundation from this knowledge transfer and accountability. Please understand there are no perfect jobs. I am saying this because I do not want you to think a career coach is going to help you find your dream job. They do not exist.

- **Hidden Jobs are NOT hidden**

Hidden jobs are non-advertised, little-known collections of newly created roles, openings and opportunities that only insiders, attorneys, accountants, golfing buddies, neighbors, alumni, consultants, service providers, managing partners, company owners, company officers, board members, board advisors, and C Suite executives know about right now. Tip: These hidden jobs are known by the people you have in your cell phone and email contacts.

- **Believe change is constant**

The hidden job you are seeking is right around the corner. "For every door that closes – there is another one that just opened, but unfortunately the hallway can be hell." Good companies always need good people! People are always getting fired, riffed, transferred, recruited, promoted, demoted, downsized, re-assigned and confidentially replaced. They can retire, die, relocate, resign or simply quit to start their own company. Subscribe to your local Business Journal and follow the news and trends about people and companies.

- **Stop being an applicant**

The world has changed, the deck chairs have been re-arranged and it is time to begin managing your professional career. Get over the unemployed syndrome. Stop telling people you are looking for a job. Instead... "You are in between career opportunities" "You are in career transition" "You are being very selective in choosing your next role, assignment or project" Your attitude adjustment starts right NOW! You are GREAT Talent for Hire! Never Settle for anything Less!

- **Adopt a new empowering identity**

"The Ultimate Power is to Know Thyself" – Socrates. You need to distinguish yourself by knowing "Your Highest and Best Use" to any organization. What is your brand, slogan, motto or mantra? Are you forgettable or memorable? Truly understand and discover your P.L.A.N.

-**Passion** (your highest and best use = expertise)

-**Lessons** (what you've learned and how you've grown)

-**Accomplishments** (your top 8 career wins)

-**Needs** (People + Challenge + Balance + $Worth)

- **Master Your Messages**

Mastering your messages involves having your resume professionally developed by an expert resume writer. We have talked about this. Develop a kick-ass and dialed-in elevator pitch and in case of an interview, be prepared to answer these questions:

-Who are you and what is your BRAND?

-Why you are in transition?

-What is your ideal organizational role?

-How are you a great fit for that role?

-What's in it for the company?

- **Develop Advocates to refer you**

Your Top 12 networking contacts need to be educated about who you are and what you do. You need to learn the correct approach on how to network like a master. Remember the old adage: "It's not what you know, it's who you know." The new paradigm is **"It's not who you**

know, it's who knows you and what they are saying about you!" This is type of advocacy that is essential for a successful career path to the C-Suite!

- **Be More Social**

The internet has changed job search forever. There are thousands of job opportunities posted on Twitter, LinkedIn, and Facebook. Social networks are untapped gold mines filled with unknown and hidden information, ideas, tips, leads, and referrals to your target contacts, companies, and job opportunities. Use the "Advanced Search" tool on LinkedIn. Optimize your LinkedIn profile to 100%, because it's the #1 search tool used by Executive Recruiters.

- **Internal Referrals Rock**

Many HR Managers and Executives (the hiring authorities) prefer getting internal referrals because once they publicize the job; they receive hundreds of emailed resumes, many from unqualified candidates. Candidate referrals from known and trusted employees is the #1 company preference when hiring new employees. So, reach out to your employed networking contacts and secure more inside referrals. It is also a good idea to connect with Headhunters. Use LinkedIn to research executive search firms and get connected to at least 50 recruiters that focus in placing executives in your industry, (products or services), your salary range and your level of management.

- **Beware of your Digital Dirt**

When I come up with a quick search of your name, what do I see? Most employers are going to do a personal, financial and professional background check just to make sure who you really are. If I scour your LinkedIn profile, what will I see? What about on Facebook and Twitter? Do I dig up digital dirt on you? What are you posting on these social media sites? You want to have that cleaned up because everybody looks at it and companies and recruiters have access to all social media sites and can see everything. That's their job, right? They're detectives in a murder mystery. Their job is to find the right candidate and make sure there's no skeletons in the closet.

Chapter 5

Keys to the Job Interview Mindset

Having a job interview mindset involves a conscious person's guide to better interviewing. In today's job market, the only job security is your ability to secure a job. What is relevant about The Interview Mindset is the fact that it works if you apply the methods and advice contained in this book.

Here is one important rule to note:

First and foremost, the interview is a conversation, NOT an interrogation! The interview is only an answer to part of the solution. We need to believe that conversation is an action step towards learning and making decisions. The only way to have meaningful conversations and creative dialogue is to ask really good questions. The critical task is to find the right questions, ones that are open-ended enough to engage anyone in a productive conversation.

There's a lot of lessons you've learned that handle a lot of potential interview bombshells that come your way, like "What's your greatest lesson?" or "What's your biggest weakness?" or "What's your most embarrassing time of your career?" If you don't answer those questions right, it's the kiss of death. If you come off as "I've never made mistakes," or "I don't have any weaknesses," that's impossible. If your ego enters the room before you physically walk through the door, you're going to get rejected right away. It's the quickest way to be rejected when the ego flies.

The question in many cases is the answer. There's no sound bite. Instead it's important to get the question right. Most of us are busy answering the wrong questions. Try answering these questions instead:

- *What are your commitments?*
- *What is worth doing? What do you love doing?*
- *Why would you hire you? What do you do best?*
- *Are you a buyer or seller?*
- *Are you a leader or a follower?*
- *How do you make a difference?*
- *What matters most?*
- *Where is the pain?*
- *What do you need to do to be successful?*
- *What didn't the last person do that you (Mr. Hiring Manager Name) really needed them to accomplish?*

What Matters Most

In every employment interview, there is always one party that likes the other party more than the other. The hiring process is like a courtship that can begin slowly and end quickly. It can also start fast and develop into a long-term relationship. Remember this: there are coincidences when it comes to interviews. Of course, you would never get an interview if there was no interest from both parties. There must be a need and a want for the process to begin. The first interview is always an interesting setup...almost like a blind date.

Do you really know your career goals? I am a firm believer that if you don't' know what you want, that is probably what you will get – Nothing! What makes you happy? If you can create the ideal job for yourself, what would it look like? How much autonomy, responsibility, and accountability will you have? Are you a people person who wants to make a difference in other peoples' careers? Are you likable?

Interview Mindset Defined

In every interview, your personal leadership qualities will be under scrutiny to a much greater extent than in previous recruitment processes. To shine, your attitude and mindset will be just as important as your technical and leadership competencies.

If you don't think you can do the job, don't go to the interview. If you think you can do the job, your behavior must demonstrate that you do.

There is no middle ground.

The logic is straightforward. If you don't demonstrate confidence in your ability to make a difference in a company, why should the "Decision Makers" (DM) have confidence in you? After all, they are making what will probably be their single most important decision - choosing the right person for the job. It's not unreasonable to expect that they might be worried about making the wrong decision and be a little risk averse as a consequence.

As a short-listed or final candidate, you start with important psychological advantages. First, congratulations, you are a short-listed candidate. You have been narrowed down from a large number of candidates and your skills and competencies must have connected with the DM on some level. You are already ahead of the game and have earned leverage.

Second, the DM desperately wants you to succeed at interview. They start each interview wanting the candidate in front of them to be the solution to the problem of finding a new employee. No executive committee or selection panel starts out with the aim of not making an appointment. So, your job as a candidate is to make sure the company has no reason not to appoint you to the position.

In short, the decision makers have got to believe that you are their next employee to be hired, and this is where the right mindset is key.

Five Types of Mindset Keys

There are five mindsets keys that I coach:

Mindset Key #1: The Doctor/Patient Mindset. When I talk about a mindset, it's kind of like they pretend that you play the doctor and the hiring manager is the patient. When you are sick and visit the doctor, he or she ask questions to determine your condition, so they can help. It's the exact same process during the interview. That's the doctor/patient mindset.

Mindset Key #2: The Consulting Mindset. Act like a consultant. You're looking for problems that require solutions. What would you do differently in an interview if you had the mindset that you were acting as a consultant? You're trying to understand what the issues are, what the problems are, because that's what a consultant has to do. They have to understand how they're going to be able to help them. By the way, that doctor/patient mindset, as you're determining whether or not they have problems, your question to them, as an interviewer, is *"What are the top five or six critical or deliverables that the person that gets this job needs to do in the next six to twelve months?"*

It's the absolute number one question to ask right out of the box when you get a chance. Then you're saying that this person needs to do that, needs to do this. You're not nominating yourself too soon because you don't know whether or not you want to do this job yet.

What if they give you menial types of responsibilities and goals that you used to do 10-15 years ago? Then that's going to be a challenging problem. You're not going to feel challenged on the job. Your job is to find out what those deliverables are and if you're really good and you're good to go with your examples and stories, you can pull one of those examples out that matches up with one of the things that they bring up as one of the greatest deliverables or issues that they need to have this person solve in the next 6-12 months.

Mindset Key #3: The First Day on the Job Mindset. Another mindset is to pretend it is the first day on the job. You're thinking to yourself, "I've got this job. What am I going to do? How am I going to act?" You'll be confident, enthusiastic, excited. You want to be in the moment and you're going to go in there and try to figure out what the boss needs done. What's keeping him up at night? What are the big objectives for the day or the week or the month that the boss needs to have completed? You're enthusiastic. Your mindset is different when you think of it going into an interview.

Mindset Key #4: Be a Buyer, Not a Seller Mindset. I love this mindset. You don't know if you want this job yet. Don't sell too soon. Don't brag too soon. Don't start crowing about your great examples and stories before you know what the heck these people need.

That's a big Sales 101 mistake, where you start doing a feature and benefit presentation before you even ask the customer what's wrong. What do they need?

You have to know that before you start delivering a solution or a remedy or answer to their problem. Buyer versus a seller. When you're a buyer, you're asking good, compelling questions like "Why would somebody want to work here?" You don't know yet. You're not nominating yourself too soon. You're asking, "What does a person need to do to be successful?" Not "What do I need to do to be successful should you bring me on board?"

Don't nominate yourself too soon. Remember — be a **Human Switzerland and Stay Neutral.** There will be a time when you need to convert over and be totally committed and ready to take on this challenge, but you have to determine whether they really can keep you motivated and is this going to be challenging? That's very important.

Mindset Key #5: Pretend You Won the Lotto Mindset. The final mindset is kind of a fun one where you drive home, and you pick up the groceries and you buy a lotto ticket and you use that lotto ticket as a prop to pretend that you've won the lotto for $500 million and you know you're going into an interview the first thing tomorrow with the CEO and the chairman of the board. Do you still go on the interview or do you not?

What would your mindset be if you pretend that you've won the lotto and go on the interview? How would you act differently? What would you say? What would you do? You know there's nothing they can say to ruin your day because you've just won. You could actually buy the company if you were so inclined.

It's an interesting mindset because now you are more relaxed. You're more comfortable. You're going to be more likable. You might even have fun because you're learning about an opportunity and what's going on in their company might be very exciting to you, but you might also think this isn't the right fit. Those are the five mindsets.

In other words, saying that you should answer a question X, Y, Z is not nearly as powerful as showing them, "Well, if you answer it wrong like this, this is what happens." Like selling yourself too soon. Some people that you may know might have started selling themselves right from the beginning and then realized that they didn't want the job at all, under any circumstances. The key is don't allow the hiring manager to think you need the job more than company needs you. Don't be aloof or act like you are interested, just keep in mind you have choices, too!

What happens is they may believe that you are desperate. Especially, if you're out of work. If you need them more than they need you, they may think, "Well, Jeez, we've got John in our back pocket. We know he really wants to work here. Bring in the next candidate, so we can compare and contrast that person with John." But if you give them the impression that you're not 100% on board, you're still determining, it's a two-way street. You've got to look at them as much as their looking at you, because these are critical decisions. These are business decisions and you cannot afford to join the company for the wrong reasons.

In fact, there are statistics that show 50% of the people that take the first job offer that comes their way, when they're out of work, 50% of the time they're looking for a new job in six months because they jumped too soon. They ignored the red flags and the yellow flags because they just wanted to get back in the ranks and get on a payroll. They settled for less and now they're regretting it and it's ten times worse now. Maybe more.

The Interview

From the first moment you set foot over the threshold of the company doors to begin an interview and selection process, your outlook and behaviors must be those of a prospective employee – not an applicant. At every stage of the selection process – during formal and informal moments – the decision makers must see you as their next employee. The key is to treat everyone you meet like they are a major customer or client you could lose. Kindness matters.

This doesn't mean that you won't have development needs, or gaps in your knowledge to fill – but it does mean that you demonstrate the outlook and behavior of someone who is already at the required leadership and management level and can communicate what it is for the employer, should they desire to hire you. Also, whatever exercises they can do to make sure they have the right mindset before they sit down with the interviewer.

Let's look at this simple statement: *Tell me about yourself.* Sounds simple, right? This is one of those "break the ice" kind of statements that open it up for a long discussion about who you are and what you represent, what makes you tick. There's a right way and a wrong way to answer that question. The wrong way is where they just go ahead and recite their resume from the time they get out of school all the way to the current job. It's boring. No one wants to hear your whole story in one two-minute answer, because it's impossible to do.

There is another strategy that when someone says tell me about yourself, you can say, "Where would you like me to start?" Let them tell you. Throw it back to them. It's okay to ask a question to a question. In an interview, if you need more info, if it's not clear, ask, "Can you rephrase the question? I'm not quite sure I understand what you're asking." But in this case, then tell me about yourself is such an open-ended question that it's fair to say, "Where would you like me to start?"

Let them be more specific. The reason they say, "Tell me about yourself, John," is because there's a lot of questions that can't be asked legally. I call it the "vomit question" because they're getting people to vomit. They talk too much. They share too much. Irrelevant things. It starts the interview off in a very awkward moment. The answer to the question is your positioning statement. It's the two-minute elevator pitch that everybody talks about. If you're not really good and it's not rehearsed, and you don't really have a good elevator pitch, well, you better have one.

The other question that everybody gets sunk on is, "Why did you leave your last job?" Or "Why are you looking to make a job change now, at this time in your career?" If you don't have an airtight answer, you're definitely going to have problems. If it's not credible, believable or understandable, then they could have that tinge of doubt throughout the whole interview because you never answered it properly. You never gave them a real reason to say, "Hey, I get that. That makes a lot of sense."

That's called the exit statement. The exit statement is, "Why are you leaving or why are you looking for a new job." If you don't answer that right, they may never let you know that they don't believe you or it doesn't make sense, or they're not sold on your answer. The next thing is they're passing on you and you don't even know why. That's a mistake that people make a lot. Probably the biggest mistake in any interview is not being ready for the exit statement.

There's so much more that goes into the works than just having a mindset when you're in an interview. You have to have a plan. There's assessments like the 22 questions I listed further in this chapter. You can self-assess yourself. You have to plan your age stories and examples. The lead up to the Interview Mindset is all well in advance before you actually walk through the door to go in your interview at the company.

It starts with the planning and the map and the trails and getting everything organized. You're not just going to start walking on your journey before you know where you're going. There's a beginning, a middle, and an end in so many ways and the end is the payoff into how to go in there and eliminate the competition.

When I talk about mindset, I'm talking about when the guy is not in an interview. Keeping his mindset on a level plane so he can do the homework and do the mock interview with a good friend or a professional career coach to prepare answers for all those questions to improve your delivery during the interview. This is where your mind has to be before you walk in the door to meet with the employer. There is a big difference between a general life mindset and the mindset that is getting ready to go on stage.

You all may have butterflies when you go into an interview, but you don't want to be scared. Two different things there. You have butterflies because you think it's a good opportunity, but you're not scared because you've done your homework. When you get that first interview, that's when it's time to go back to school and really study. You got to book it! You have to be ready. You've got to learn who you are. You have to know what your plan is, what your answers will be. What are your passions? What are the lessons you've learned? What are your accomplishments and what are your needs?

The Bookend Answer Approach

This approach is a great way for you to frame your answer. When somebody says, "Why should we hire you for this job?" You say, "I believe you should hire me for this job because…" That's the front side of the bookend and then you deliver your content answer in the middle. Reflect on your top eight competencies that you can frame sentences around, paying particular attention to the top three to five key attributes or characteristics that demonstrate your qualifications, strengths, abilities and competencies. And when you finish that answer, you bookend it by saying, "That's why I believe you should hire me for this job."

The beautiful thing is that they hear it three times. They say it once, they hear you say it one time at the beginning of the bookend, and then they hear it again at the end of your answer. It's a positive reinforcement type of thing and it works. You don't want to do it with a question like, "What's your greatest weakness." "Oh, my greatest weakness is..." and then you tell something, and then you say, "That's my greatest weakness." You don't want to emphasize a greatest weakness with the bookend approach.

This system has worked for me several times. The book-ending is a good way to start, and then you don't just drop off a cliff trying to end your answer, you come to the end of it, and then you very confidently say, "That's why I believe you should hire me for this job."

The "tell me about yourself" question is an open-ended question that is designed to get people to go off on tangents, talk about their life, their family, their upbringing, their schooling, their current relatable activity and their most recent job. The problem is the "tell me about yourself" is known as the vomit question because people don't know where to start. They don't know what to say sometimes. They're not prepared, and they just start talking about themselves and they volunteer stuff that is irrelevant to the conversation.

The proper answer is a positioning statement, which is known as what? The two-minute elevator pitch. It's essentially, who are you? What's your highest and best use, and what are your greatest deliverables, that you believe are invaluable to a company? It's a description of what you were meant to do in your career, and what you enjoy doing, and what you delivered, and how you get things done. Your method, your steps, your processes, and make it personal. This is the first, maybe the second question out of the box for most interviews, especially a phone screen over the phone because companies want to get you talking.

If you start reciting your resume, it's really not going to get you any more points. In fact, you should never recite the resume unless the interviewer actually asks you to. "Tell me about your first job out of college and bring me up to the current time as we speak in your most recent job." If they say that, then you do it in two minutes or less.

The answer to the positioning statement is essentially most relevant info that is probably within the last three to five years. Who you are, what you've become, what you represent, how you make a difference. Your passion for what you do. The satisfaction and reward of performing incredible accomplishments and achievements in your current or former role with the company you work for, or previously worked for.

This could be done in two minutes or less without a lot of rambling. As long as it's a scripted statement, and you memorize it, and you practice so it sounds unrehearsed. And there could be varying lengths. That could be a 30 second, a one minute, a one minute thirty seconds, it's up to them to determine how much information they want to share that gets the interviewer comfortable with the answer.

Mock Interviews

To exercise your mind, it is ideal to hold a series of mock interviews. You should do a mock interview with somebody who has done this before. Not just your spouse or brother or your sister but somebody who is a neutral contracted third party. A professional career coach is a good choice. They are there to help as an independent contractor that's going to be honest on how you did. They are going to be direct. They're not going to pull any punches when they need to really let you know, "You can't say that," or "You know what? You're coming off a little too egotistical," or something like that. Those are the things that people don't do.

The interview practice is extremely critical. No actor would go on stage without rehearsing a dozen times. It's the most important meeting of your life. You shouldn't be winging it. Then we've got the actual interview itself, but we also have a section on networking to get you to the interview.

When I'm speaking, or I run my meeting, I have a show of hands when I ask, "How many people have gone through a professional mock interview training session?" Maybe 3 out of 30 people raise their hand. I say, "Folks, you got to think about this. If your son or daughter has a big final exam at school tomorrow morning, are you going to say go ahead and kick a soccer ball or shoot some baskets or are you going to have them go upstairs and suggest they really get ready for the exam?"

It's the same thing with you. It's probably even more important because you have to get that job offer to make ends meet with your family. Are you going to go into the interview with the CEO or the owner of the business and wing it? Or are you going to go to the bar or go to the bowling alley tonight? What are you going to do? You're going to get ready for that interview. Why not do a mock interview and be ultimately prepared? The ultimate preparation for a job interview is to be ready to eliminate the competition. Not just separate yourself but eliminate the other people who are competing for the same job. If you're not that well prepared, then someone else is going to get the offer. Pretty simple.

You eliminate the competition by performing really well during your mock interview and then this translates to doing well in the main interview. It's the power of visualization and manifestation.

When you do a mock interview, you see how well you are doing in a practice session in light of the fact that you are going to make mistakes. There's no judgment calls but when you do fumble through an answer, you have to go back and get critiqued. You fix, and you update, and you make it perfect. You have to be ready for the tough ones that come your way.

Here are some sample questions. Try them out and get a professional to tell you how well you did!

22 Tough Interview Questions with Answer Strategies

1. Tell me about yourself?

Just talk for two minutes. Be logical. Start with college or your first job OR ask, "Where would like me to start?" The interviewer is looking for communication skills, and linear thinking, so bear in mind that seemingly innocuous question such as "Tell me about yourself" is actually, "Why are you the ideal candidate for this position?" The best answers are honest, confident, and concise. Also, score a point or two by describing your major attribute. Hint: Use your Positioning Statement.

2. Why are you leaving your current position? Why did you leave your last job?

This is a very critical question. Don't "bad mouth" your previous employer. Don't sound "too opportunistic." Best to relate major industry problems, a buy-out, shutdown, re-org, or downsizing. Also good is to state that after long personal consideration, a chance to make a contribution is very low due to company changes. Hint: Use your Exit Statement.

3. What do you consider your most significant accomplishment?

This can get you the job. Prepare extensively. Score points. Tell a two-minute story, with details, and discuss personal involvement. Make the accomplishment worth achieving. Discuss hard work, long hours, pressure, and important company issues at stake. Most importantly, tell them "HOW" you did it. You must create a value perception before the meeting has ended!

4. Why do you believe you are qualified for this position?

Pick two or three main factors about you and your job that are most relevant. Discuss for two minutes with specific details. Select a technical skill, a specific management skill (organizing, staffing, planning, leadership), and a personal success attribute to mention.

5. Have you ever accomplished something you didn't think you could?

Interviewer is trying to determine your goal orientation, work ethic, personal commitment, and integrity. Provide a good example where you overcame numerous difficulties to succeed. Prove you're not a quitter, and "that you'll get going when the going gets tough."

6. What do you like/dislike most about your current/previous position?

Interviewer is trying to determine compatibility with open position. If you have interest in the position, be careful. Stating that you dislike overtime or getting into details, or that you like "management" can cost you the position. There is nothing wrong with liking challenges, pressure situations, opportunity to grow, or disliking bureaucracy and frustrating situations.

7. How do you handle pressure? Do you like or dislike these situations?

High achievers tend to perform well in high-pressure situations. Conversely, the question also could imply that the position is pressure packed and out of control. There is nothing wrong with this as long as you know what you're getting into. If you do perform well under stress, provide a good example with details giving an overview of the stress situation. Let the interviewer "feel" the stress by your description of it. Use a "Philosophy + Real Life Example" answer approach.

8. The sign of a good employee is the ability to take the initiative. Give me an example of where you have demonstrated initiative?

A proactive results-oriented person doesn't have to be told what to do. This is one of the major success attributes. To convince the interviewer you possess this trait you must give a series of short examples describing your self-motivation. Try to discuss at least one example in-depth. The extra effort, strong work ethic and creative side of you must be demonstrated.

9. What's the worst, or most embarrassing, aspect of your business career? How would you have done things differently now with 20/20 hindsight?

This is a general question to learn how introspective you are and to see if you can learn from your mistakes. If you can, it indicates an open, more flexible personality. Don't be afraid to talk about your failures, particularly if you learned from them. This is a critical aspect of high potential individuals.

10. How have you grown or changed over the past few years?

This requires thought. Maturation, increased technical skills, or increased self-confidence are important aspects of human development. To discuss this effectively is indicative of a well-balanced, intelligent individual. Overcoming personal obstacles or recognizing manageable weaknesses can brand you as an approachable and desirable employee.

11. Why would you hire you? (What are your most significant strengths?)

Be prepared. Know your Top 8 Competencies. (Your career acronym) Create a passionate sentence for every strength. Select those attributes that are most compatible with the job opening. Most people say "management" or "good interpersonal skills" in answer to this. Don't, unless you can describe the specific characteristics of management (planning, organizing, results, hiring and staffing, etc.) and/or how your relationship skills have proven critical to your success. Use a "Book-end Answer" approach.

12. What do you consider your most significant weaknesses?

Don't reveal deep character flaws. Rather, discuss tolerable faults that you are working towards improving. Show by specific example how this has changed over time. Better still; show how a weakness can be turned into a strength. For example, how a concentration on the details results in higher quality work even though it requires much overtime.

13. Deadlines, frustrations, difficult people, and silly rules can make a job difficult. How do you handle these types of situations?

Most companies, unfortunately, face these types of problems daily. If you can't deal with petty frustrations, you'll be seen as a problem. You certainly can state your displeasure at the petty side of these issues, but how you overcome them is more important. Diplomacy, perseverance, and common-sense can often prevail even in difficult circumstances. This is part of corporate America, and you must be able to deal with it on a regular basis.

14. One of the biggest problems is _____. Can you describe your most comparable accomplishment? How would you implement this task or project?

Think on your feet. Ask questions to get details. Break it into sub-parts. Highly likely you have some experience with the sub-sections. Answer these and summarize the total. State how you would go about solving the problem, if you can't answer directly. Be specific. Show your organizational and analytical skills.

15. Give me an example of when you executed a project flawlessly?

The ability to get the job done regardless of obstacles that come up along the way is a key trait of top performers. Failure to execute is one of the top reasons people fail. Be ready to describe another great story or example that demonstrates your competencies.

16. Tell me about your biggest team directed accomplishment in a

difficult time or situation?

Top performers get the job done by utilizing the talents of others. No one can do it all. Top performers know this and leading a team is something they are good at. Relating a strong example of your leadership skills is a strong predictor of future performance.

17. How do you compare your technical skills to your management skills?

Many people tend to minimize their technical skills, either because they don't have any, or they don't like getting into the detail. Most successful managers possess good technical skills and get into enough detail to make sure they understand the information being presented by their group. Try for a good balance here if you want to be seriously considered for the position.

18. How has your technical ability been important in accomplishing results?

Clearly the interviewer believes he needs a strong level of technical competence and resourcefulness. Most strong managers have good technical backgrounds, even if they have gotten away from the detail. Describe specific examples of your technical wherewithal, but don't be afraid to say you are not current. Also, you could give an example of how you resolved a technical issue by "accelerated research."

19. How would you handle a situation with tight deadlines, low employee morale, and inadequate resources?

If you pull this off effectively, it indicates you have strong management skills. Be creative. An example would be great. Relate your toughest management task, even if it doesn't meet all the criteria. Most situations don't. Organizational skills, interpersonal skills, and handling pressure are key elements of effective management. Good managers should be able to address each issue, even if they were not concurrent. Deftly handling the question is indicative of your skills, too.

20. Are you satisfied with your career to date? What would you change if you could?

Be honest. The interviewer wants to know if they can keep you happy. It's important to know if you're willing to make some sacrifices to get your career on the right track. Degree of motivation is an important selection criterion.

21. What are your career goals? Where do you see yourself five years from now?

Most importantly, be realistic! Blue sky stuff brands you as immature. One or two management jumps in 3-5 years is a reasonable goal. If your track indicates you are in line for senior management in 10 years, it is okay to mention. However, if you've had a rocky road, better to be introspective. Hint: Use your Professional Objective Statement.

22. Why should we hire you for this position? What kind of contribution would you make?

This is a good chance to summarize. By now you know the key problems. Re-state and show how you would address. Relate to specific attributes and to specific accomplishments. Qualify responses with the need to gather information. Don't be cocky. Demonstrate a thoughtful, organized, strong effort kind of attitude.

Be Prepared

Now that you are armed with some likely questions, do a two and a half to three-hour mock interview and go through every one of these questions. For my clients, I go over this with them. Together we break down and tweak their answer after each question. If they nailed it and they did a really good job, then we say don't change a thing, that's perfect. Now they know. Peace of mind that they've got that answer without any problem.

But if they need to work on it and they need to get their frame of mind and they want to get used to saying whatever they are going to say, we can play it back and do it again and see how well they do the second time around. The goal is correcting any evident issues and things they are not comfortable saying or it comes off as negative. I'm also looking at their eyes, and the tone of their voice, their body language, facial expressions. Neurolinguistic Programming (NLP), which is the study of non-verbal communication, is really important.

On the other hand, a lot of people in hiring, like human resources, are aware of NLP, and some of them are practitioners and certified, so they can tell when somebody's making it up, or telling the truth. It's in the eyes and in the tone of their voice. Those things are reviewed, and I bring them up in case they're not really giving me good eye contact and they're tentative in their tone of their voice. If they end on a high note, I get a little concerned that they're not really comfortable giving the answer. It's almost as if they're seeking approval like, "Is that the right answer, Mr. Hiring Authority?" Whereas, if they end on the down note, it is a lot more authoritative. It's a lot more credible, believable and understandable.

These are the little things that they couldn't do on their own and wouldn't know unless there was somebody with them as they were role-playing and doing a mock interview. Basically, the tough questions are, "Why did you leave your last job? Or, "Why are you looking for a new job?" And the answer needs to be a very well-crafted exit statement. The exit statement is known as the **Reason For Leaving or Looking (RFL).** It can be a catchall and they want to know what the motivation is for making a job change, or what happened in their last assignment or job.

Recruiters always want to know the reason for leaving or looking. What's the motivation behind the job search? Interviewers are going to ask that question, they want to see, they want to look in their eyes, and that answer can sink or swim any candidate. You need to be honest when answering these questions.

If you don't answer it convincingly, with credibility, believability, and it's understood, meaning if it's confusing or they dance around the answer, or they don't get to the real reason, well, now there's doubt. When doubt creeps into the RFL, you've got a problem. The interview may not go very well. You may never recover if you don't handle the RFL. You've got to cover it really well.

What I have created here is more of a visual, a formatted approach to the RFL. It's an Oreo cookie. Oreo cookies as we know, have three parts. You've got the top chocolate part of the cookie, the white stuff in the middle, and the bottom part of the cookie. And this is how you format and structure the RFL.

The top part of the cookie has to be a positive statement. It starts out like, "In my last assignment with ABC Company, I really enjoyed working with that company over a period of X years. I've made some incredible accomplishments and made some incredibly great professional friendships. However..."Now this is the stuff in the middle. "However, over the last year, we lost two of our biggest clients, the company was put up for sale, they reorganized, the new hiring CEO came in with his own team. It totally affected the impact of my role within the company, and my position was eliminated." Then, the bottom part of the cookie is another positive statement. "That said, this has given me a fantastic opportunity to explore new companies such as yours, Mr. Hiring Authority at ABC company, where my background, expertise, and wisdom will have mutual benefits with your needs and the company's vision, growth, and plan for the future." Something that is going to resonate with them. They need to really capture the whole gist of the statement.

It needs to be scripted out first, then rehearsed, and they need to be able to replay it in an unrehearsed way. This is not that difficult, as long as you practice. But when it sounds like a script, and you're robotic in the way that you're reciting something, it doesn't come off as authentic and genuine as it should. If you're comfortable reciting your own answer, the Oreo cookie formatted RFL, then they'll be comfortable. If you sound uncertain, if you sound like you're winging it, if you sounded like you're making it up as you go along, it's not going to work. Y you need to be really, really good at delivering the RFL, or you'll never get into the important part of the interview, which is, "What have you done in your last job or assignment? More importantly, **HOW** did you do it?" Whatever that significant example is, focus on the impact you made.

Chapter 6

The Likability Key

Let's say that this one individual is interviewing against three or four clones of him or herself. Seems like they all have the same background, number of years of experience, same education, they make the same amount money. Why would they hire you over the other three candidates? What's the final decision-making criteria? The answer is likability. If you're all equal across the board with three or four other candidates, the one they like the most, the one that fits and matches with the existing team that will blend well will be the one that they make the offer to. It happens every time.

It's an absolute. They're not going to hire someone they don't like. Whether they can do the job blinded or an arm tied behind they're back, they're always going to go with the one they really like the most. "I really like John. Jeez, what a great guy and, yes, we believe he can do the job. Make him the offer." That's what happens.

Things You Should Not Do at an Interview

Don't try to steer conversations as a job seeker. You need to slow down and let the owner or the leader or the CEO lead the conversation where they want to go. I believe there's two types of interviews: a personality interview and a performance interview. You really don't know which one you're going to get.

When you go to the first interview and you're interviewing with the CEO or the owner of a company, you have to feel that out. You have to let them take the leads. You have to figure out if they just want to have a nice, warm get-to-know-you meeting, or do they want to get down and dirty and intense to find out whether or not you can perform the duties as a job.

I had a client who went into a lunch meeting. This meeting would normally give you the impression that this is going to be a get-to-know-you meeting. This is a public place and the candidate immediately starts leaning into the owner. The candidate starts asking about all of the details of the corporate vision. He asks, "What the goals and what's working, not working and what have they tried that's failed?" The owner of the business just wanted to have a good sandwich and get to know the candidate; who he is, what he is thinking and what's new in his life. That was his only plan for the meeting. He ended up getting rejected because the owner said the candidate was too intense. The feedback was clear - the owner wasn't ready to be smothered. "It was simply an exploratory interview and I wasn't ready to address corporate objectives and issues about my company because I just wanted to have a get-to-know-you lunch with the guy."

That was a big mistake and the minute the candidate left the meeting, he knew he blew it and his chances of landing that role were slim to none. He called me and said, "I screwed up." Things did work out for him because he ended up running a company in Ohio and now he's the president and CEO and he learned a good lesson from that meeting. God gave you two ears and one mouth...shut up and listen, engage, repeat and engage. By all means, don't try to control the conversation with the hiring manager.

Listening skills are very important. Listen and respond. In the very beginning, you have to let that person who is thinking of hiring you for their key position steer the boat. Do not take over the tiller. Do not step on the throttle. You've got to just roll with this. You're deciding whether you like this guy just as much as he likes you. You're hoping that he likes you.

You should also note that no answer for an interview should ever exceed two minutes in length because people don't have the attention span to listen that long. When this happens, the message gets lost because you've gone on and rambled. They forget what you said, or they don't take enough notes, and then they can't remember. Rambling is another kiss of death.

You must also make sure that you don't give them the impression that you need them more than they need you. That's another possible pitfall for job seekers. They go in and they just insert themselves into the job too soon. There is a time to do that, but you have to wait. You must understand what's really going on here. We're trying to figure out: Where are the issues? What are the pains? What are the things that need to be accomplished for the person that gets this job? I say the person that gets this job, you don't nominate yourself too soon.

I always tell my clients, act like a **Human Switzerland.** Be neutral. Be very neutral in the beginning. You don't want to declare that you're the best guy for the job until you figure out what needs to be done. Is that really what you want to do for the next five years? Like going to the doctor. You're sick, you go to the doctor and the doctor must ask questions to discover the route of the problem. Right? How long have you felt this way? What are your symptoms? What medication have you tried? Is there any history of illness in your family?

It's the same exact thing in a job interview, but the mindset is the job seeker, the candidate interviewing for the role, is the doctor. The hiring authority is the patient. It's the responsibility of the job seeker candidate to find the pain, find out what's wrong, what are the goals, what's not happening, what have they tried that's not working? Maybe even ask a really good question like, "What didn't the last person do in this role that you really needed them to accomplish?" This is how the Doctor-Patient Method Interview Works.

Doctor-Patient Interview Method

Note: This mindset is introduced in Chapter 5.

Much like a doctor asks a patient probing questions during a visit to a physician's office, you need to ask excellent and compelling questions during an employment interview. When you are sick, and you go to visit your doctor he may ask several questions like: How do you feel? What are your symptoms? How long have you felt like this? Have you had this problem before? Have you been taking any medications to alleviate the problem and has this remedy helped in the past?

When you are speaking with a prospective employer in the job interview a good way to understand the company's "real needs or (severe) pain" is to ask questions, much like a doctor does to a patient before he makes a diagnosis for the problem and prescribes/provides the medicine, remedy or solution.

When given an opportunity to ask a question during an interview, here is the first important question to ask:

"Mr. Hiring Manager, what are the top 5 or 6 critical objectives that the person that gets this job needs to do or accomplish in (3, 6, 9, or 12 months) in order for you to feel you made the right choice or hire?"

Don't nominate yourself for the job yet! It might not be the right match for YOU! Be quiet and wait for the answers! Even if it takes a while for the hiring manager to get to the real issues, problems, obstacles or "severe pain." If he or she only gives you 1 to 3 objectives, ask "What else? Is that all there is?" Make sure you get 5 or 6 critical objectives or "deliverables" that determines a successful candidate's performance during the first year! Write down or memorize each objective and during the meeting you need to address how you have achieved similar goals by describing "HOW" you did it with on-the-job examples! Then, if you are able, tell "HOW" you might go about implementing and organizing the specific tasks and objectives.

Tip: If the hiring manager has difficulty answering, it may cause you to wonder if they know what they really need. So, keep trying to understand HOW severe is their pain? You must probe with the following question as long as you understand the reason "why" the position is open.

"What did you want the last person (who had this job) to achieve that he or she failed to do?"

The **Doctor-Patient Method** works if you keep this mindset throughout the phone call, interview or consultative meeting. Make sure you ask the same questions to everyone you meet at the company during the interviews...because things can change, and you may get different answers and/or viewpoints.

This is going to arm the job seeker with some pretty good information. They market themselves by telling their own anecdotal story, which is one of the things they need to be prepared to do. I say you must have a minimum of eight different big win stories that you're very proud of that you need to be able to address throughout the interview.

Almost like a **Human Jukebox**. You got to be ready at any given moment to pull one of those stories and replay that story like it was yesterday. The story format needs to include a challenge, action, result, or example of one of your big wins or successes that you've done recently. Not 20 years ago, but relative to what's going on today.

When asked a question, I suggest that you have a two-part answer ready to go. Your first part is your philosophy. What is your philosophy on the question? In this case, pressure or deadline. How do you handle those? You have to say something that is pretty matter of fact. You don't just say, "Yeah, I know how to handle pressure really well." You say, "You know, John, I believe high achievers should be able to perform well under pressure."

It's a beautiful statement. It means those are the kinds of people you like to work with. Those are the people you look and gravitate towards hiring for your own team and, oh by the way, that's you, too. It's all-encompassing, but here's where people fail. They forget to back it up with a story when they were really, REALLY, under pressure. I want to hear about the compelling nightmare that's happening or the evil of doom that's cascading down the mountainside towards the company front door.

You don't have to win an academy award, but you really do need to draw your listener in to say, "Jeez, how is Mark going to get out of this mess?" This is all done in less than two minutes. You don't have to go on and on. The story needs to be concise. It needs to be a real reason for the actionable item or the actionable methods or processes that you use to solve problems and then what was the final result? Challenge, Action, Result. The C.A.R. statement -

(Challenge + Action = Results)

Chapter 7

Networking Works

At Hire Consulting Services we say, *"Your Network is your Net-Worth!"*

Networking is the lifeblood of the job search campaign and if you don't like it, it's going to take you longer, because what's the alternative to networking? It's sending your resume into the black hole, which is the internet, and hope the phone is going to ring. You'll be waiting until doomsday.

There is something called a networking interview or an informational interview. It is nothing new, but a lot of people don't talk about it often, especially when it comes to job search. An informational interview is an interesting type of meeting because you're going to meet somebody over lunch or coffee and they just think that you're networking, but what you're going to be doing is really putting on a good performance, almost as if you're in an interview. So, they get excited about you and they feel comfortable and confident about you because you've now pulled your story. Long story short is that they feel, "Like they can introduce you to someone at the company who would want to meet with you."

Ultimately, you need to be ready to eliminate the competition should you be going up against three or four or five other people for the same job. Part of the goal with the interview training that I do is being able to eliminate the competition and get the offer. What you do with the offer is a different strategy. That's negotiating the optimum job offer. Networking skills are used by successful people to market themselves, generate business, and to solve problems every day!

Preparation for a Networking Event

Learn everything you can about the event such as activities, attendees, schedules and so forth. Then determine what will make you feel comfortable. Should you go with someone you know who's also attending? Is it appropriate to bring a friend, associate, or client? Would it be more profitable for you to be an attendee or an exhibitor?

A convention is a great opportunity to strengthen existing relationships and expand your network. Think about who will likely be there and make a mental note of the new contacts and reconnections you want to make.

Participation at a Networking Event

- **Get Involved**

One way to put yourself at ease is to give yourself something to do. Volunteering not only gives you a job to do, but gets you involved and naturally connects you with other volunteers and participants.

- **Focus on Others**

Rather than worrying about what you're going to say, focus on what others are saying. When you have your attention on something or someone other than yourself, your self-consciousness will disappear, and others will be more likely to remember and appreciate you.

- **Listen and Gather Information**

Good conversationalists know the importance of listening. It conveys a natural interest in others and enables you to be more aware of what to say and talk about in order to keep the conversation flowing.

- **Use People's Names**

    Pay attention as people introduce themselves so that you can address them by name during the current conversation and increase chances of remembering their name at a later date.

- **Move on Graciously**

A networking event is a place to meet and mingle. Yet, people often feel uncomfortable ending a conversation, so they mingle and talk with others. Just be gracious, with a closing comment such as "Nice to meet you. Have a good afternoon." "Good luck with your new venture."

- **Exchange Business Cards**

Business cards are best exchanged when there's some stated reason to do so, such as "I'll call about scheduling a time to get together for lunch" or "Give me your card and I'll send that information to you tomorrow."

- **Relax, Have Fun and Enjoy Yourself**

People often get uptight about attending networking events because they feel they have to find a new prospect, make a sale, or accomplish some significant goal. Networking is meant to be fun. Relax. The more at ease you feel, the more likely it is you'll make some good solid contacts. The goal shouldn't be the quantity of interactions, but the quality.

Networking is a natural process of meeting people, making contacts, and building strong professional relationships. It is not a difficult process, yet it is a deliberate process. As humans, we have a natural need to be in relationship with others. It is up to each of us to honor that natural desire to connect, link, and develop camaraderie. There are endless possibilities all around you -- people are just waiting for someone to break the ice. Your network can be your most valuable accomplishment in your life.

You've got the planning, the execution of the plan, which is networking

networking, and then you've got the interviewing and closing the deal. And then finally there's new job assimilation and onboarding coaching that I provide.

The Golden Rule of Networking: *"People will connect with and refer opportunities and their important contacts to those people they know, like and trust."*

- Remember: **It's all about THEM - Not You!**
- Invest 99.9% of the conversation with that person asking questions about themselves and their career and business.
- The average person knows about 250 people – think about it- Who are the most powerful, most successful and most connected people you know?
- Every time you talk with someone, ask eight little words: **"Is there anything I can do for you?"**

The Secret Formula for Networking Success

The formula for **N**etworking **S**uccess is based on your **H**uman **C**apital (what you know) times your **S**ocial **C**apital (who knows you) times your **R**eputation (who trusts you and what people say about you).

NS = HC x SC x R

Chapter 8

Keys to Salary Negotiation

Before you say "Yes"

Before you accept an offer, know:

Your particular needs for choosing the right company. What are your passions? What are your lessons that you've learned? What are your accomplishments, which are story examples, and what are your needs? The needs are people, challenge, balance and worth. Those are the four criteria to rank to determine whether or not this is the right company for you to go to work with, accept their job offer and join that company.

People are important. That always has to be number one. You have to really like them. They have to like you. You have to be able to learn from them. They have to be able to learn from you. You want to be inspired by these people. You want to know they've got vision. They're all onboard. If you're the sharpest arrow in the quiver, it's going to be a long, long ride. You are not going to like it very well if you're the sharpest arrow in the quiver or the sharpest needle in the quill and they're all looking up to you for the answers and you're around a lot of people that are just lost. You are not going to like that job and you're going to be looking for a new job in six months or less. There is also no chance for you to grow there.

I always say it's got to be the most challenging type of opportunity for you to really want to get out of bed in the morning because your bank account does not get you out of bed. Your balance in your checking account does not get you to not hit the snooze alarm. It's the motivation. It's the challenge, the charge, the "can't wait to do this and make a difference in the world," that you really got to love what you're doing to get out of bed in the morning. Money is a stimulator. Not a motivator. This is a fact. When offers are being done, offers are not there to motivate people to accept the job and go to work. The money is put on the table to stimulate them to accept it. Then the negotiation is a whole different thing, but people challenge and then balance. Balance is work-life balance. No mystery here. Some people want to work to live. Some people live to work. Know this before you say yes.

Does your plan sit well with the company? Some companies expect 70 hours a week, like a New York law firm, and then others want you to go home after 40 hours. If you're a soccer Saturday mom or dad and you've got to be up and taking kids to soccer games or picking them up after school, well, your work-life balance is different than the guy that's an empty nester or the lady, the mom, that's no longer managing a family, where they can jump on a plane tomorrow morning to Albany, New York and be happy doing it without causing trauma in the family.

Work-life balance is an important state of affairs you need to know before saying yes. That changes as we all mature and grow older and our kids grow up and raise families of their own. That's another criteria. Is it going to be disruptive in your life? Are you going to be able to embrace the company and do what they need you to do? In fact, there are statistics that show 50% of the people that take the first job offer that comes their way, when they're out of work, 50% of the time they're looking for a new job in six months because they jumped too soon. They ignored the red flags and the yellow flags because they just wanted to get back in the ranks and get a payroll. They jumped too soon. They settled for less and now they're regretting it.

Then the final criteria, which is always going to be number four, is can they afford to pay you what you're worth based on your contribution? People, challenge, balance and worth and when you get into negotiations, it's a whole other chapter there. You definitely want to have the negotiations while the offer is still on the table. How you respond to the first offer and the whole negotiation process also matters.

The 5 things everyone wants from their job... but you can only get 3 consistently *By Chris Lord – Founder, Bridge Builder Coaching*

Here are 5 criteria for job happiness. The catch is that you will probably only be able to achieve three of these consistently in your "ideal" job. Which three are the most important to you? Which two are you willing to sacrifice?

1. Live where you work

2. Love who you work with

3. Love what you do

4. Work reasonable hours

5. Make good money

Criteria Notes:

1. Are you willing to get on a plane every week, week in and week out to do what you love? Do you hate to commute but are fine with being on an airplane to travel for work? Then you don't need to live where you work vs. someone who hates driving 1 hour to work for a job.

2 and 3. "Love" is intentional in these two criteria. Not like, not enjoy, but really **love.**

4. "Reasonable hours" are how you define it. If you love what you do, 60+hours per week may be reasonable.

5. "Good money" is how you define it. You may work for the Forestry Service, earn $50K per year and think you're overpaid. Or you may work on Wall Street and earn $1M per year and it's never enough.

Negotiate the Optimum Salary Package

For years I have coached many executives through successful negotiations like the dialogue examples below. To make it even easier, I've broken it down into 4 easy-to-follow steps.

Step One: Try to Delay the Salary Topic

Note: In some states it is now illegal to ask what your prior salary was. But, just in case you are asked what your salary requirements are by an HR Manager or Hiring Manager try to delay the conversation until the offer is made. If they ask you your salary requirements during the interview, or on a phone screen, say something like this:

"My number one priority now is to learn more about your organization and this role to determine if I'm the best match for your needs. Should an offer be extended, I'd be happy to negotiate with you at that time, and I'm confident we'll be able to reach an agreement."

This usually takes the conversation away from salary. However, if they insist on talking about it at that point, ask them to disclose the company's range first.

Step Two: Find the Salary Range for Your Role

Why find the range? Well, you don't want to offer something too high and make the employer think they can't afford you. On the other hand, you don't want to offer something too low and miss out on a larger paycheck for yourself.

It's best to handle this by saying something along these lines:

"I'd be happy to negotiate with you. First, I'd like to have an idea of what the company has budgeted so I can negotiate within that range. What salary range is the company looking at?"

Saying this will ensure you can make a proper offer that is fair to both parties.

Step Three: Make a Ranged Offer

When you do disclose your offer, always give them a range and not a specific number. Come prepared with a range to quote. That range should be something that you know is realistic for that position and that you would be comfortable accepting if they offered you. You can find baseline information on Glassdoor and Salary if you are unsure.

Step Four: Know Your Comfort Zone

Always have your ideal number and your "deal breaker" number that you will not accept. When you are accepting a position that pays less than you currently make, you can handle this by saying:

"Of course, compensation is important, but it's not my only priority right now. I'm more concerned about finding a position that I can enjoy and grow in. If an offer is extended, I'm confident that we can reach a fair agreement on a salary that works for both parties."

This helps keep the dialogue open for when for when it comes time to negotiate fully.

Executive Negotiating Statements

What do you say when you are asked for your salary requirements? Remember, the company needs to make an offer for you to evaluate it - Not the other way around!

Know your numbers in advance. Determine what do you really NEED and what do you really WANT?

Your (demands = requirements) responses could be any of or a combination of the following:

• "I think salary is a very important topic, and I would be more than happy to discuss it once a mutual interest has been established." (Get back to discussing your accomplishments)

• "Your company has a very good reputation, and I'm sure the compensation package will be fair enough to keep me motivated and productive." (By the way, what is the salary range for this position?)

• "Based on my accomplishments and contributions, I would like to be paid at the same level as other executives of my tenure and caliber." (What is the salary range for a person of my caliber?)

• "Regarding compensation, I am flexible and willing to negotiate, once we have developed a mutual interest." (Get back to discussing your accomplishments)

• "If we decide that I am the right person for this job, I am sure we will be able to come to an agreement on compensation." (Get back to discussing your accomplishments)

• "At this time, I am most interested in determining if I am the right person for this job. If there's a fit, I'm sure salary won't be an issue." (Get back to discussing your accomplishments)

• "Are you making me an offer? (If so, what salary range did you have in mind?)" Only use this response later in the process.

Second and/or Final Round Negotiations

Go back to the Hiring Manager (not Human Resources) and say:

• "This is a great opportunity and I am excited about working with you (or) joining your company."

• "I am inclined to accept your offer; however, there are 3 (or more) items I want to discuss (negotiate) with you."

• "If we can reach an agreement on these items, I will be prepared to accept your offer today." Remember, if you ask for something and receive it – you need to give something in return. That's how deals are made.

• Always try to conduct this negotiation "in person" if possible!

• 80% of the outcome of your salary negotiations will be determined by your optimistic attitude and accurate assumptions!

• Remember, everything is negotiable and get everything in writing!

Job Offer Checklist

1. Job Title

2. Position reports to

3. Start Date

4. Salary (monthly or bi-monthly pay periods)

5. Performance Review Date
    • 6-month early review?

6. Commission structure

7. Bonus
    • Eligibility? % Company Performance vs. Individual Performance
    • Possible for pro-rate bonus for a portion of first year?
    • Guarantee a portion of first year's bonus

8. Signing bonus
    • Verbally indicate it is to make up for lost bonus/stock options, etc.

9. Vacation weeks /Paid Time off / Maternity leave
    • Extra weeks rather than higher base?

10. Health Insurance
     - Effective date
     - Monthly Premiums/Co-Pay/Annual deductible

11. Retirement: Matching 401K

12. Stock options, Profit Sharing, Equity

13. Company Car or Monthly Allowance

14. Travel and entertainment expenses

15. Club membership

16. Executive Coaching

14. Relocation Expenses
     - Temporary housing
     - # of trips home
     - House hunting trip(s) with spouse
     - Real estate fees
       a) selling end - pickup 5% - 7% commission? Points?
       b) buying end - closing costs
     - Packing & moving household goods
     - Discretionary amount for miscellaneous expenses
     - Gross-up taxes

15. Trailing Spouse Career Transition Coaching Assistance

16. Separation/termination Agreement
     - 6-12 months full salary and family health benefits

17. Employment Offer/Acceptance Contingencies
     - Drug Test/Physical exam
     - Verification of college degree
     - Employment References
     - Background Check
     - Financial Credit checks
     - Behavior assessments

18. Offer Letter reviewed by employment attorney

Chapter 9

New Job Assimilation (Onboarding)

The First 90 Days on the Job

There are a lot of things that can go wrong in the first 90 days, even after you've done all this hard work. You've done all this interviewing. You've done all the networking. You've negotiated a pretty good salary! You better go in there and hit a home run and not piss people off, because you're going be under the microscope for the first 90 days. That's a given! The company's hoping they've found the right person and hired the right guy or girl for the job, right? You have to prove them right! Your job is to prove that they made the exact right choice, otherwise that ship's going down, okay? Nobody likes a loose cannon. You know what the definition of a loose cannon is? You know how it works? Have you ever heard the reason where that term came from?

It was during the old wooden ship days during pirates and early times and they had cannons onboard and if a big squall came up and the boat started rocking, those cannons were flying around if they were not chained down to the deck. So, if they start rocking and the cannons are rolling, one of those cannons is going to fall through the floor and sink the whole boat, and everybody dies. That's the definition of a loose cannon. You don't want to be that!

New Job Assimilation

In today's breakneck business world, companies demand fast results from every newly hired executive. The traditional long-term "honeymoon" period is a thing of the past. "Hit the ground running," is everyone's mantra. "Faster, cheaper, better, 24/7." That first 90 days, you're under the microscope. Everybody wants to be satisfied that they've got the right person that they hired.

Almost everyone can tell a story about a highly intelligent, skilled executive who was promoted to a key leadership position only to fail in the job. While poor hiring practices or poor cultural fit may cause some failures, by far the greatest number are due to poor assimilation of the executive into the team or organization.

According to a report conducted by the Wall Street Journal, there are five general reasons why executives flop in their new jobs. The study concluded that a misstep in any one of the following areas often resulted in a "house of cards" effect:

1) Confusion or lack of clarity about what their bosses expect of them.
2) Failure to build partnerships with peers, subordinates, and direct reports.
3) Inability to identify and achieve their top three "most important" objectives
4) Lack of political savvy within the organization
5) Taking too long to learn the job

Problems, which lead to ineffective leadership, can be expensive to correct. The most obvious cost, a severance package, translates into two or more years' salary. Problems such as qualified staff jumping ship, diminished morale, poor strategic positioning, missed opportunities, and tarnished reputations, while less obvious can result in survival issues for the company.

Many cost-conscious organizations are recognizing the value of having executives get started on the right foot. To speed assimilation, and prevent early missteps, companies are using a strategy of one-on-one executive coaching. A personal coach can help the new executive quickly identify job-related competencies that are necessary for success.

Working with the coach, the new executive can develop a targeted improvement plan to fill any identified gaps.

An executive coach can assist a new executive in several other areas as well:

- Rapidly gaining an understanding of the overall "big picture" and what is truly valued.
- Establishing solid people relationships with managers, peers, and team members.
- Identifying "themes," establishing priorities, and developing visible deliverables.
- Spotting possible obstacles, and how they might be overcome.
- Communicating the guiding vision, issues and priorities, and proposing thoughtful, informed actions.

This quick start approach for executive assimilation has the benefit of eliminating "trial and error" assumptions, developing solid alliances with essential stakeholders, learning to respond to new situations in conformity with what already exists and establishing a solid basis for a successful future with the organization. By engaging an executive coach, companies can provide their senior management teams the most useful tools to increase their effectiveness and sense of accomplishment.

Give yourself the best chance of succeeding in a new role. It is important to realize that assimilation is a two-way process. Successful new hires take ownership of and responsibility for their assimilation into a new company and don't just leave this in the employer's hands.

Assimilation does not begin only on your first day at a new company. It starts during the interview and the recruitment process. While the initial objective is to get the job, it is equally important during this period to assess what it would really be like to work for the company; how people act in the workplace; how employees communicate with one another; and how the work gets done.

Building relationships

Critical to the success of assimilation are the relationships developed at the beginning of a new hire's tenure. Look to build relationships inside and outside the company and to develop coaches, sponsors, mentors and confidants. These relationships will also develop an interest in you and have a vested interest in your success.

Joining a new organization should be an enriching experience as you have the opportunity to start afresh and not repeat past mistakes. As part of your assimilation, build trust and demonstrate that you are trustworthy. If you say you'll do something, do it. Volunteer to get involved or help others and recognize other people's efforts. Do not self-promote; but do keep people appropriately informed as to what you're doing. Be a receptive listener, willing to accept feedback.

Have a plan

Develop a plan to map your assimilation and your progress towards targets. Identify thirty-, sixty- and ninety-day plans. Plan to learn, develop and execute upon your arrival. Study the company history and learn the business. Get to know the market and your competition and link this knowledge to your role and responsibilities. Measure your progress against your plan and ask others for feedback. It is important to realize, too, that although your first 90 days will probably be the most formative, assimilation never really stops and, as your environment changes, you should apply your assimilation principles throughout your career.

Assimilating into Your New Position

- Read the new corporate culture.
- Build alliances and influence others.
- Determine and align expectations.
- Focus on early impact projects.

Maintaining Your Career Momentum

- Continuously survey your professional environment.
- Occasionally redefine your professional objective.
- Always have a communications strategy.
- Manage your professional reputation.

Focus on Others

Rather than worrying about what you're going to say, focus on what others are saying. When you have your attention on something or someone other than yourself, your self-consciousness will disappear, and others will be more likely to remember and appreciate you.

Listen and Gather Information

Good conversationalists know the importance of listening. It conveys a natural interest in others and enables you to be more aware of what to say and talk about in order to keep the conversation flowing.

Use People's Names

Pay attention as people introduce themselves so that you can address them by name during the current conversation and increase chances of remembering their name at a later date.

Successful assimilation strategies take into account the time limitations of today's business world by helping the new leader focus on the best use of their time and talent during this crucial early phase. They create a plan to facilitate quick action for long-term success. A results-based follow-up measurement and feedback process is used to determine the impact of the leader's business objectives. High-impact assimilation goes beyond just creating a plan and provides ongoing support to get the most sustainable success out of the plan. This process helps keep the leader on track when the "real deal" surfaces and adjustments are required based on new challenges that were not clear at the time of hiring or emerged since then from the rapidly changing world of work.

Typically included in an assimilation strategy is a development plan that surfaces the "skeletons in the closet." If delegating was a problem in the past, it is time to start focusing on how to offset or strengthen that competency, rather than waiting until you're settled into your new job. After all, things rarely settle down enough so that you can focus entirely on your development. To succeed, executives need to make development an ongoing process.

Be Popular at Work

For years we've heard that it's more important to be respected than liked. Yet study after study is proving conventional wisdom wrong, finding instead that the road to success is more often a series of popularity contests.

Research at Columbia University shows that jobs, pay raises and promotions are more apt to be awarded based on a worker's charisma than on his or her academic background or professional qualifications.

Outplacement firms have found that during corporate downsizings, hiring and firing decisions boil down to how well people are liked by their supervisors. It's not enough just to do a good job, you must be likable in the eyes of your employer.

The good news is that being likable is a skill that can be learned.

When people encounter you, they subconsciously ask themselves four questions to determine whether they like you as a person. First, they seek friendliness. Then, they ask themselves if you are relevant to them. Next, they ponder whether you have empathy for them. Finally, they ask themselves if you are 'real'- that is, authentic and honest. If the answers to those four questions are affirmative, you receive a high Likeability Factor."

Here are four steps to increasing the "L Factor."

Step One: Increase Your Friendliness

Your friendliness is a function of your ability to communicate openness and welcome to others. Make an effort to greet people cheerfully, smile often and adopt a friendly mindset that you communicate through positive body language and words.

Step Two: Raise Your Relevance

Your relevance has to do with your connection to others' interests, wants and needs. The more relevant you are, the more people like you. Relevance has three levels:

- Contact. The odds are, your "L Factor" will increase with "functional distance," such as sitting next to someone at a party or living nearby.
- Mutual Interests. Having common interests or experiences makes people feel validated and generates a sense of community and personal respect.
- Value. Relevance is strongest when the value you offer meets another person's wants and needs. This produces positive attitudes in the person's mind and contributes to your allure.

To become more relevant, find ways to connect with the interests and needs of others. Know what they're passionate about outside of work.

Be aware of their emotional needs and willing to respond to them.

Step Three: Show Empathy

Your empathy reflects your capacity to see things from another person's point of view and to experience his or her feelings yourself. When you connect with someone's feelings, and they believe you're "with them," it delivers a psychological hug. Ask yourself, do I:

- Know how that person is feeling about his or her life situation these days?
- Understand what it must feel like to perform the person's tasks day after day -- be it caring for an elderly relative at home or managing a heavy workload?
- Share the same emotions about key issues?

By making yourself more emotionally available, your connection with people - and your likable factor - will grow dramatically.

Step Four: Keep It Real

Realness is consistency between your beliefs and actions. To be true to yourself and others, you need to:

- Do what you want to be doing in life.
- Live with purpose.
- Commit to the principles of your work.
- Be the same person on the outside as you are on the inside.
- Be direct and honest with others.

The more you live by your values, the more your perceived realness will elevate. Conversely, if people decide you're not real, they will discount your friendliness, relevance and empathy - and probably dislike you. Being likable comes down to creating positive emotional experiences in others. When you make others feel good, they will tend

To gravitate to you.

Closing out Your Job Search

Closing out your search means ending other negotiations that may be pending with other companies and contacting any recruiters you may have been in contact with to let them know where you can be found in the future.

It also means communicating with your network of contacts to thank them for their help and to express an interest in staying in touch with them. You worked hard to building and maintaining your network of contacts. It is way too valuable to lose. Decide whom you want to keep in your network long term. Develop a strategy so that you regularly stay in contact with them.

Here are a couple letters to consider using to communicate your announcement to the people that helped you along the way:

Job Landing Announcement Sample Letter #1

Dear _____,

Thank you for the time and assistance you provided me during my job search over the past few months.

I would like you to be among the first to know that I accepted a position as [Your Title] for [New Employer], a national firm headquartered in Cincinnati, Ohio. I will be providing the direction to expand the company internationally and am especially excited to traveling the globe once again.

Please let me know if there is anything I can do you in the future.

Once again, thanks for all your help and advice....

Job Landing Announcement Sample Letter # 2

Dear _____,

I would like to share some very exciting news with you!

I have just accepted a position as [Your Title] with [New Employer]. The position offers an opportunity to put my [your talent] skills to work for an organization that truly values people who create and communicate.

I am deeply grateful for the role you played in making my career change a success. The information, leads and support you gave me are appreciated. You will recall that it was your suggestion to network with my financial association colleagues that eventually led me to this job opportunity. I was often reminded during the past few months how easily we can lose contact with old friends. Now that we are back in communication, I hope that will not happen with us.

Keep in touch...

Chapter 10

Keys for Working Smarter, Not Harder

Are you working longer hours but getting less done? Are you being asked to do more in less time? Beginning to feel like a hostage at work? Productivity problems can make you feel incredibly stressed - and then you're just spinning your wheels. But wait! There is help. You can use your mind. You can soon be winning the mental game of personal productivity. Peak-performing sales professionals work smarter, not harder. They want to achieve to the maximum in business and then go play. Here's how you can do that too:

1. Start the day being very clear about what you want to accomplish - both personally and professionally.
2. Once a quarter, perform a time analysis on your entire week - both at home and at work.
3. Make a list of the things you should completely avoid doing today - and then don't do them.
4. Don't strive for perfection in everything, as perfection doesn't matter with all tasks.
5. Sweep your mind clear of clutter before you engage your brain on a project.
6. Set boundaries and limits for yourself so you position yourself for balanced time management.
7. Schedule "real-life" personal appointments in your organizer or daily planner in advance and adhere to them.
8. Ask yourself, "Am I managing my time well enough to allow me freedom to enjoy life after work?"
9. At the end of the day review what you have accomplished, and compliment and reward yourself for good tasks completed.
10. Motivate yourself for good work by promising yourself exercise or a break reward once you achieve a level of excellence in a task.

11. Stay conscious of your time management choices during the day.

12. Compartmentalize your tasks so you focus on one task at a time.

13. Build up mental momentum with each successful task completed so you proudly gain energy as you go through your day.

14. Build variety into your schedule so you have interesting activities to look forward to during less exciting tasks.

15. Create positive tension and an urgency to get things done faster by having more to do than you can actually achieve - but keep your focus in the here and now.

16. Don't classify too many things as priorities or as urgent - be selective.

17. Know what to say no to and stick to your decisions.

18. Continually ask yourself, "Is this the best use of my time?"

19. Visualize yourself succeeding before every task. Hint: Start with the end in mind!

20. Don't be continually reactive to your electronic tools - don't reflexively retrieve them when they come in. Collect voicemail and email at specified times to maintain uninterrupted focus.

21. Plan quiet time for thinking, planning and analyzing.

22. Create your own custom "best time management program" - don't use someone else's.

23. Ask yourself, "Is what I am doing right now really making a difference?"

24. Do things today that will give you leveraged advancements in your work-weeks from now.

25. Systematize regular, repetitious tasks by setting up smarter processes.

26. Build in delegation and support from associates, friends and family to take pressure off yourself.

27. Lower your expectations of perfection and don't expect 100% completion of your to-do list each day - carry some over for another day.

28. Review your values every quarter so you know what is important to you, and how to plan your time.

Winning the mental game of personal productivity is all about being intentional in the planning and execution of your day. It's about using the superior powers of mind you possess to creatively solve the daily challenges you face so you maximize your value every moment. Master the mental strategies on this list and watch your productivity soar.

The Essential Keys of Executive Leadership

1. If you don't know the answer, learn to say, *"I don't know"*
2. It is easier to get into something than to get out of it.
3. If you are not criticized, you may not be doing well.
4. Look for what is missing. Many know how to improve what's there; few can see what isn't there.
5. Presentation rule: when something appears on a slide presentation, assume the world knows about it and deal with it accordingly.
6. Work for a boss for whom you can tell it like it is. Remember, you can't pick your family, but you can pick your boss.
7. Constantly review the developments to make sure the actual benefits are what they were supposed to be.
8. However trivial your early assignments may appear, give them your best efforts.
9. Persistence or tenacity is the dispassion to persevere in spite of difficulties, discouragement, or indifference. Don't be known as a good starter and a poor finisher.
10. In doing your project, don't wait for others: go after them and make sure it gets done.
11. Confirm the instructions you give others, and their commitments, in writing. Don't assume it will get done!

12. Don't be timid: speak up, express yourself and promote your ideas.

13. Practice shows that those who speak the most knowingly and confidently end up with the assignment to get the job done.

14. Strive for brevity and clarity in oral and written reports. The key to great communication is brevity.

15. Be extremely careful in the accuracy in your statements.

16. Don't overlook the fact you are working for the boss. Keep him or her informed. Whatever the boss wants, within the bounds for integrity, takes top priority.

17. Promises, schedules and estimates are important instruments in a well-run business. You must make promises – don't lean on the often-used phrase: "I can't estimate it because it depends on uncertain factors."

18. Never direct a complaint to the top; a serious offense is to "cc" a person's boss on a copy of a complaint before the person has a chance to respond to the complaint. When interacting with someone outside the business remember that you are always representing the company.

19. When interacting with someone outside of the business remember that you are always representing the company. Be especially careful of your commitments.

20. Cultivate the habit of boiling matters down to the simplest terms: the preverbal "elevator speech" is the best way.

21. Don't get excited in engineering emergencies: keep your feet on the ground.

22. Cultivate the habit of making a quick, clear-cut decision.

23. When making decisions, the "pros" are much easier to deal with than the "cons". Your boss wants to see both.

24. Don't ever lose your sense of humor.

25. Have fun at what you do. It will be reflected in your work. No one likes a grump… except another grump.

26. Treat the name of your company as if it were your own.

27. Beg for the bad news.

28. You remember a third of what you read, half of what people tell you, but 100% of what you feel.

29. When facing issues or problems that are becoming drawn out, "short them to ground."

30. When faced with decisions, try to look at them as if you were one level up in the organization. Your perspective will change quickly.

31. A person who is nice to you but rude to the waiter – or to others – is not a nice person. (This rule never fails.)

32. Never be afraid to try something new. Remember, an amateur built an ark that survived a flood while a large group of professionals built the Titanic.

To me, the keys of great leadership boil down to:

- Your Confidence
- Your Dedication
- Your Integrity
- Your Trust
- Your Love
- Your Respect

www.HireConsulting.com/resources

Chapter 11

HCS Career Coaching Service Descriptions

When in doubt – Hire a Career Coach. The HCS Four-Phase Campaign Strategy™ is a complete campaign which encompasses four distinct phases and over 30 distinct action items. Following a focused strategy allows for the greatest opportunity that the best possible career position is landed as quickly as possible. The four phases are: Campaign Prep, Marketplace Communication, Interviewing and New Job Assimilation. Let's take a brief look at what's involved:

Phase 1: Campaign Prep

Executive Skills, Competencies and Behavior Assessments: The biggest predictor of executive-level performance is general cognitive ability. Right alongside cognitive ability is behavior. HCS uses The Predictive Index© to give each client a running start on understanding their own needs, drives and behaviors to interview more effectively, secure the offer, land the job and exceed expectations in their new role.

Resume and LinkedIn Development: Are you not getting the type of response from your resume and LinkedIn profile that you expect? We will correct errors, rewrite weak passages, tweak the formatting, wordsmith and offer insightful comments and suggestions to ensure that your resume passes the "Who cares - So what?" test. The well-developed resume and "optimized" LinkedIn Profile are critical job search success and the blueprint for the perfect job interview.

Create a Job Search Marketing Plan™ (JSMP): Simply said, this is your job search strategy! During this session your coach will help create a Job Objective, Positioning Statement (referred to as a 2-minute elevator speech) and Exit Statement (reason for leaving your job). This session will help you assess your competencies and create examples of career accomplishments. Additionally, you will define exactly what you are looking for in the next job and develop a list of target companies you are interested in pursuing.

Phase 2: Marketplace Communication

Secrets of Professional Networking: This session is designed to help you learn the art of building relationships for the purpose of acquiring and disseminating information; it can be done informally and naturally every time you interact with another professional. When you network, your objective is to learn about the other individual and to seek his or her advice on your project. In the case of job searches, the project is about locating resources - including individuals - that will help you learn about the job market specific to your particular expertise and interests.

Utilizing Executive Recruiters: One of the biggest mysteries of job search is, "Why recruiters never return my calls?" This session will help you understand how to work effectively with Headhunters. The greatest chance of success still comes from your own network of acquaintances, business associates, etc. However, search firms are constantly handling assignments, which are not publicized or perhaps even known outside of the executive office.

Phase 3: Interviewing

Mock Interview Training: This 2-hour session is customized to your specific situation and concerns. We coach and guide you in identifying and expressing your strengths, skills, competencies and value as they relate to an employer's needs. We'll also help you deal with perceived problem interview questions, help you with your presentation, positioning statement, and exit statement to help you separate yourself from the competition during face to face and phone screening and mock interviews.

Salary Negotiation Coaching: We'll help you develop a sound negotiating strategy, learn when it's most advantageous to discuss salary issues, and become skilled at keeping the discussion focused on what's really important and away from too-early discussion of compensation. This could be the most valuable investment you make during your job search!

Phase 4: New Job Assimilation

New Job Assimilation Strategies: This session will provide great advice and strategies to help you start the next job on the right foot. It's very important to keep people, who are part of your network, informed about your job search success. Let them know when and where you finally accept a job. And stay in touch after you start your job--you don't know when you'll need that network again. Remember, you influence people around you all the time. Your actions, words and conversations affect the way others may choose to think or act. Choose wisely. It's your responsibility to be a positive source of influence in your new job environment.

HCS Career Transition and Management Coaching Services

HCS coaching has been used with great success to guide hundreds of clients from the various fields of business. Most of the coaching is done via telephone and email. The regular, consistent and ongoing contact through email will help clients get the support they need and will help encourage them to discuss issues/problems they are having throughout the job search process. We work with clients throughout the United States and internationally via webcam with Skype. Some of these customized services include:

- Pre-scheduled weekly 1-hour telephone or face-to-face office meeting sessions.
- 24-hour Email response on an ongoing basis Monday-Friday.

- Just in time 90-minute return phone call response time – Monday-Friday.
- Safe and confidential coach and client relationship.
- Access to extensive resources, articles and content to help with professional and personal development.
- Practical tools including: strategies, feedback, discussions, listening, perspective, validation, communication, solutions, planning, structure, resources, options, and mock interview training.

When you work with HCS Career Management Services, you will receive the following customized job search campaign training and support:

- Training each client to seek out opportunities that happen from skilled networking.
- Assessing each client to discover the "Highest and Best" use to future employers.
- Packaging and presenting their skills that will maximize their marketability.
- Investigating the hidden job market for opportunities that are not currently published.
- Developing the key elements about the art of networking.
- Professional resume and cover letter development.
- Online access to recruiters, company databases for researching target industries and companies.
- Introducing ancillary resources that will give you the competitive edge.
- Recommending event activities and associations that will expand their connections.

Conclusion

In Today's Market, Job Security is the Ability to Secure a Job!

At Hire Consulting Services (HSC), we strongly believe in providing an engaging, highly interactive career coaching program that will result in positive economic and emotional outcomes.

We assist executives and professionals in career transition to cope with the anxiety and stress of job search by rebuilding their confidence, identifying their key strengths, targeting areas of knowledge and work that they enjoy, and giving them a feeling of self-worth.

We also believe that there are four required areas of expertise that C Suite executives must have for success: Experience, Personal Beliefs and Values, Network Clout, and Quality Relationships.

For executives looking for an improved alternative to the traditional outplacement program, HCS Career Management Services offers unique and customized support whereby we guide and educate every client on how to conduct a professional job search campaign.

Our program is not developed around mass email, mail campaigns or directionless networking. It is based on:

- Creating a strategic job search campaign,
- Making relevant contacts and connections,
- Researching and studying companies and industries that are likely matches for the talent of our clients, and
- Executive coaching and career transition mentoring to help land in short order and find a position that has a positive fit.

Being a career coach *and* an executive recruiter has allowed me to provide a very unique perspective to the people I have coached. I excel in coaching business professionals and executives who are changing jobs, contemplating starting their own businesses, or job seekers who are currently in career transition. I deliver a proven structure and process, coupled with honest expert advice to help you execute your job search campaign strategy to ensure your next career move is the one you want.

In addition to regular cast members with positions like CIO (chief information officer), CFO (chief financial officer), CMO (chief marketing officer), COO (chief operating officer) and of course CEO (chief executive officer), here are a few new team members of the C Suite:

Chief Customer Experience Officer
Chief Automation Officer
Chief Innovation Officer
Chief Relationship Officer
Chief Intellectual Property Officer
Chief Data Officer
Chief Privacy Officer
Chief Compliance Officer
Chief Human Resources Officer
Chief Administrative Officer
Chief Learning Officer

Hire Consulting Services provides a no-cost phone consultation to assess your personal career situation and determine if career transition coaching is right for you. Contact HCS by phone: 760-230-4301 or email: info@HireConsulting.com and please include the best days and times that you're available to talk by phone and send a brief description of your situation along with your cover letter and resume. We'll get back to you with a good time to schedule the appointment.

*We are here, ready, willing and able to help you Navigate and Execute Your Executive Career Path Success with the **Keys to the C Suite….***

Happy Hunting!

Mark S. James

Bonus Chapter

Learnings From Landing
(Executive Testimonial)

My name is Mike Elnisky. I was vice president of sales and marketing, which isn't who I am, but what I was doing. I had a P&L of $250 million, 120 people in my organization and a team of 15 people that I was personally leading. It was a big job and I was doing really well. My calendar often looked like a Tetris board, and I had two administrative assistances keeping me in line. I was in demand from 4:00am to 8:00pm. Since I ran a national sales organization, I was taking calls from coast to coast at all hours of the day.

After 17 years at one organization, due to budget cuts, I was offered a "transition", so I took it. I received a generous severance. However, it was an interesting thing because the anxiety that I felt wasn't necessarily related to money, although it felt that way at the time. It turned out it was more about the transformation of my identity and the lack of it. I went from 17 hours a day with 120 people, emails and demands, to absolutely zero. It had been the first time in my life that I had gone to a screeching halt like that, and it was terrifying. I went from being a super-star to a "nobody." Frankly, I was embarrassed and a little bit mortified.

The company gave me access to an outplacement service, but it was very cookie cutter and boilerplate services. They had a playbook and said, "Here's what you need to do. Network, send out your resume, contact your contacts." For me, it wasn't enough. There were these components of the transition that they clearly didn't address and didn't try to. There was this emotional piece to it of pushing through the fear factor of seeing the world from a place of scarcity, as opposed to abundance. That's where I was, and frankly, I was frozen. I was going through the motions and I was a zombie. In addition, I just expected the phone to ring. "Of course you're going to hire me. I'm Mike Elnisky. I'm fantastic." But guess what...nobody called.

This went on for a couple of months and their process just wasn't working. It wasn't until I went to an ExecuNet meeting in Orange County that things finally came into place. It was there that I met Mark James, and after talking with him I had an epiphany: there's a humility that has to happen if you're going to be successful in transition. I had executive coaches in my career, and still use them, and I thought, "Why am I not doing that with one of the most important decisions/times in my career and life?" So, I hired Mark.

Mark helped me realize that people in transition need to know that it's okay to ask for help. Most executives, throughout their careers, help others, and I know very few of them that don't help others, so this is the time when it's okay to ask for a favor, and be comfortable with it. Part of it is being comfortable asking people for help, but part of it is listening, and being able to be coached. I was still in this place of fear that was less about money and more about my identity. I remember thinking "I'm going to hire Mark, and then I'm going to listen and I'm going to do exactly what he says, because I don't know what the hell I'm doing." Now, I know how to sell, and everybody says that transition is just like sales. So, I'm thinking, "Okay, if I know how to sell then I know how to do this." Wrong! The commodity you're dealing with is yourself, and you have these cognitive biases that you've got to get through, and you need somebody to tell you, "No, that's B.S. This is the right thing to do." So, I was going to listen and give in to the process, and I think that was the key for me. I realized that I had to trust Mark and the process, and then just follow it tooth and nail.

I dove right in and became more of a giver than a taker because I realized that I had to do this, or else I was going to be doing the same thing over and over with no results. I got to a point where I started to connect with people and was constantly in the car driving to another event. Mark had me set up some metrics for myself: go to five networking events a week and have two coffees a day. Coffee was meeting somebody for the first time, spending 30 to 45 minutes with them and understanding their story and how I could help.

Very quickly I realized: (1) I had transitioned, and I was in a better place, but I still had this massive amount of anxiety and energy and I had to channel it into something, and (2) I realized something about me - I was successful in my career, but my values are such that I get a much higher satisfaction helping others. It's just part of who I am, and it became really clear during this period how important that was to me. So, I just went with that.

I had a great coach in Mark, so I was probably in a better position than many other executives in transition were. Before long I started to meet people and we'd go have coffee. I'd tell my story and I would learn theirs, and they would end up trying to use my network to help them connect with people that were in our circle, and vice versa. For example, a friend introduced me to the CIO at Applied Medical because we had the same values. We never worked in the same industry, we never connected, we had no other connection other than I had known somebody else in transition and she said, "You and he have the same values, so you should meet."

So, we met. As I stood up from the table after having coffee with him, I started hobbling. He asked what was wrong and I told him that I started kickboxing. He said, "You know, it's funny you said that, because I do CrossFit and I work out with the President of my company. It never dawned on me to connect you. Would you like to meet him?" I said, "Sure, why not." Then sure enough, he connected me with the President of Applied Medical, and after a few weeks of meeting and talking with other people there, they offered me a job. Because I was sore from working out, it connected us in a different way. He saw me from a different perspective, pulled me into his life and said, "Oh, by the way, I know somebody." It was just the serendipity of a networking session playing out. I ended up not taking that job, but it taught me a lot about building a network, having a story, giving to others, and having the right strategy.

In life we try to find both money and time. The goal is to figure out how to have both. Most of the time it's a tradeoff. We often focus on what we don't have and that's what I was doing until I found Mark, which was focusing on, "Hey, I don't have an income, what am I going to do?" I was living moment to moment, as opposed to taking this time to step back and see the bigger picture, which is this is a moment in my life that I actually have an abundance of time. At mid-age and mid-career, as an executive, I'm probably never going to have that again, so I should probably honor and recognize that. Because I had a strategy, it gave me the ability to think from a higher viewpoint.

I think one of the keys that I got out of this whole process with Mark was helping me organize and get a process in place. This way I could stop worrying about operating every day so that I could focus on the big picture: where I was in my life, who the people were that gave me energy, and how to put more of them in my life. Basically, how do I use this abundance of time in a way that's truly meaningful to me? Once I got there, transition became a pretty cool thing.

People find this hard to believe, but career transition is going to be a truly incredible learning moment or time in someone's life, where they can reflect back on. I sympathize with others who've had these long-duration tenured employed careers, where they've never had to look for a job, and suddenly, they're on the outside looking in, and they have no idea how they got there. If they don't have somebody to help support them during that realization or that revelation, then they can go into a deep state of denial where they start believing that they've passed their prime or they're no good anymore. They wear their transition like a scarlet letter.

Once in a coffee shop, I saw someone and asked, "Are you looking for a job?" The guy laughed and said, "How do you know?" My reply was, "Because you look like it." I could feel the negative energy coming off from him. Here he was, a professional looking middle-aged guy, sitting in a Starbucks at 10:30 a.m., in front of a computer in jeans and just not looking right. He looked like he did not belong there. Now I am more sensitive to it; job seekers who have their head buried in the job postings are extending the time to find work, because they isolate themselves from their network. Part of going out and finding a job is getting out of the house, attending events and following up with people to meet them for coffee to tell "your story." This is what it's all about. Creating an advocate to be your eyes and ears. Help them help you to provide formal introductions and referrals to their high-value connections in your target companies. I want to be around people with that optimism and positive attitude, which are exactly the type of individuals I want to hire for my team!

Currently, I'm in a position right now where I'm trying to find eight sales reps. I must have done 50 interviews in the last four weeks. So, I know. I can almost tell within 5 minutes of being in the room whether that person's going to move on or not because of the energy they give off. Some people in transition can transmit a bad vibe about themselves, as opposed to a virtuous one. So, having a coach like Mark to help work that off and get you in the right frame of mind is super critical.

Thank you, Mark, for giving me my life and career back.

About the Author

Mark S. James, CPC is the Founder and President of Hire Consulting Services. He founded HCS in 1999 and has been providing career transition coaching services and executive recruiting for over 20 years. Mark is a Certified Personnel Consultant, awarded to him in 1998 by NAPS, the National Association of Personnel Services. Mark is also a Certified Partner with Predictive Index, a behavior assessment focused on employer talent selection and employee team management.

Prior to starting HCS, he served as Senior Vice President of recruiting for four years with The Angus Group, the oldest and one of the most respected retained search firms in Cincinnati, OH. In 2002, Mark formed an ongoing strategic partnership with Centennial, Inc., another respected Cincinnati search firm, where he created and developed a very successful career transition coaching practice for senior executives and professionals.

His passionate, hands-on leadership and communication style, coupled with his honesty, integrity and drive are the core foundation on which he has built successful business relationships with the many clients and companies he has served. Since 2005, Mark has been the host and facilitator of the Southern California ExecuNet Networking Meetings for executives in career transition in San Diego and Irvine, California. He has a successful blog, ***The Career Catalyst*** and has been published in several news articles, books and newsletters, conducted numerous seminars, career workshops and public speaking events.

To learn more about how Mark James and his company Hire Consulting Services can help you excel in your career search, contact him directly at (760) 230-4301 or visit his website at **www.HireConsulting.com**.

96202261R00067

Made in the USA
Columbia, SC
23 May 2018